D1520870

Texas Women and Ranching

Women in Texas History

Sponsored by the Ruthe Winegarten Memorial
Foundation for Texas Women's History
Nancy Baker Jones and Cynthia J. Beeman, General Editors

The following individuals and organizations helped
make the publication of this series possible:
Ellen C. Temple
Leadership Women
Texas Historical Foundation
T. L. L. Temple Foundation
Devorah Winegarten

Texas Women and Ranching

*On the Range,
at the Rodeo, and in
Their Communities*

Edited by Deborah M. Liles and
Cecilia Gutierrez Venable

TEXAS A&M UNIVERSITY PRESS
COLLEGE STATION

This paper meets the requirements of ANSI/NISO Z39.48–1992
(Permanence of Paper).
Binding materials have been chosen for durability.
Manufactured in the United States of America

Library of Congress Cataloging-in-Publication Data

Names: Liles, Debbie M., editor. | Gutierrez Venable, Cecilia, editor. |
    Cummins, Light Townsend, writer of introduction. | Porter, Amy M., author.
    | Porter, Amy M. Tejanas and Ranching.
Title: Texas women and ranching: on the range, at the rodeo, and in their
    communities / edited by Deborah M. Liles and Cecilia Gutierrez Venable.
Description: First edition. | College Station: Texas A&M University Press,
    [2019] | Series: Women in Texas history | Includes bibliographical
    references and index. |
Identifiers: LCCN 2018045369 (print) | LCCN 2018047388 (ebook) |
    ISBN 9781623497408 (ebook) | ISBN 9781623497392 |
    ISBN 9781623497392 (cloth : alk. paper)
Subjects: LCSH: Women ranchers—Texas—Biography. |
    Ranchers—Texas—Biography. | Women ranchers—Texas—History. |
    Ranchers—Texas—History. | Women in the cattle industry—Texas. |
    Ranch life—Texas—History.
Classification: LCC HD9433.U63 (ebook) | LCC HD9433.U63 T38 2019 (print) |
    DDC 636/.010925209764—dc23
LC record available at https://lccn.loc.gov/2018045369

Cover: *Stampede* depicts a cowgirl wrangling bulls with her trusted dog. Artwork by
Donna Howells-Sickle, a member of the National Cowgirl of Fame. For more
visit https://www.donnahowellsickles.com/

To all the women who were, are, will be,
and could be cowgirls

And for Ruthe and Debra Winegarten,
who made this world a better place.

Contents

Illustrations

Acknowledgments

This anthology began with small talk at a meeting of the Texas State Historical Association and emerged from a symposium, Women Ranchers in Texas, held on June 2 and 3, 2016, at Midwestern State University (MSU). We are indebted to Leland Turner, who organized the symposium, Francine Carraro, director of the Museum of Art at MSU (sponsor of the wonderful reception), and the MSU office of the Provost and MSU History Department, symposium sponsors. We thank our keynote speaker, Carolina Castillo Crimm; our luncheon speaker, Diana Vela, associate executive director for the Cowgirl Hall of Fame; and the participants: Lisa Neely, Jean Stuntz, Leland Turner, Alex Hunt, Jack Becker, Dottie Ewing, Marisue Potts, and Brooke Wibracht. We especially thank the contributors to this anthology, Light Townsend Cummins for his introduction, Vicki Cummins for her suggestions, Alex Mendoza for his map, and Chase Liles for image assistance.

Special thanks go to Donna Howell-Sickles for the cover art. Donna was inducted into the National Cowgirl Museum and Hall of Fame in 2007 for her artwork that celebrates ranching women.

We are extremely grateful for Jay Dew, editor in chief of Texas A&M University Press, who not only attended the symposium but also agreed to publish this book. Finally, we thank Nancy Baker Jones, Cynthia Beeman, Melissa Hield, and Kay Reed Arnold, all of the Ruth Winegarten Memorial Foundation's Women in Texas History Series, and Joyce Gibson Roach.

Books don't just happen, and time spent producing one is time taken from something or someone else. We thank our husbands, Jake and Mike, and our families and friends for their love and support.

Cecilia Gutierrez Venable and Deborah M. Liles
May 2018

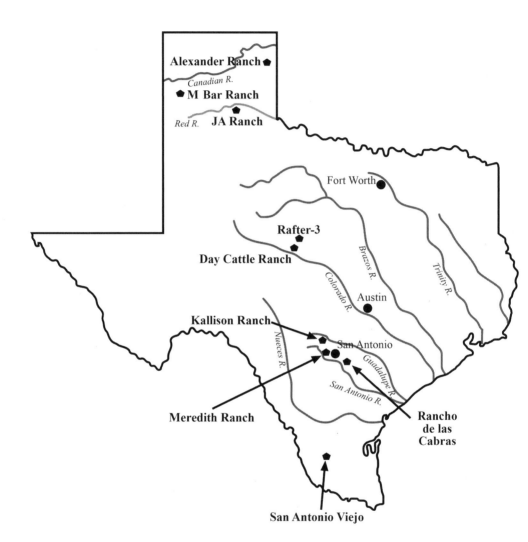

Alexander Ranch

Canadian R.

M Bar Ranch

Red R. **JA Ranch**

Fort Worth

Rafter-3

Day Cattle Ranch

Brazos R.

Trinity R.

Colorado R.

Austin

Kallison Ranch

Nueces R.

San Antonio

Guadalupe R.

Meredith Ranch

San Antonio R.

Rancho de las Cabras

San Antonio Viejo

Texas Women and Ranching

Beyond Women, Oxen, and Texas

Light Townsend Cummins

Texas has attracted a steady progression of interpretive writers and chroniclers whose publications first appeared during the Spanish colonial period. They continued documenting their observations through the Mexican era and have tirelessly recorded their impressions of the Lone Star experience all across the decades of Anglo-American domination down to modern times. Many of those who have written about Texas in a nonfiction literary vein as a place apart, starting with Fray Agustín de Morfi in the 1700s, have focused on its unique and colorful nature as a geographical phenomenon different from any other. Their pens have recorded interesting stories that touch upon the exceptional landscape, the volatile weather, the hardships of frontier life, and the inimitable human spirit that eventually resulted in the modern state we know today. Some of the best writing of this genre can be found across the nineteenth century in the works of Vicente Filisola, Mary Austin Holley, George Wilkins Kendall, Frederick Law Olmstead, John C. Duval, and John Henry Brown. Nimble writers of the twentieth century, including J. Frank Dobie, Roy Bedichek, and Mody Boatright, among others, continued this tradition of chronicling Texan traditions and its heritage well into the era of television. Some of the most iconic clichés of Texas historical memory have flowed from the observations of these commentators as they captured in their writing the folk life and folklore of the state in an impressionistic manner rooted in the uniqueness of place. Whatever the differences in their orientations across time, the literary heritage they created shares an almost universally consistent treatment of women. Female Texans are largely absent from their observations, and, perhaps worse by current standards, when they do appear they are presented in such a constricted, stereotypical fashion that women have one-dimensional existence. This is true even in the case of early women writers about Texas, including Mary Austin Holley and Melinda Rankin. For them, Texas was primarily a male phenomenon, with women juxtaposed against the interpretive reality of patriarchy. A well-known comment voicing this juxtaposition between men and women in the Texas heritage is attributed to late-nineteenth-century chronicler Noah Smithwick. He wrote in his 1900 book *The Evolution of a State or Recollections of Old Texas Days*: "Texas is a heaven for men and dogs, but a Hell for women and oxen."

This viewpoint continued into academic teaching of the history of the state. Although it would be difficult to pinpoint the exact beginnings of professional historical scholarship about Texas, most students of the state's history would agree that George Peter Garrison ranks at the forefront of those who founded the discipline in this state. His stature as a founder of Texas academic history from his faculty position at the University of Texas at Austin during the late nineteenth and early twentieth centuries is confirmed in the name of a present-day building on the UT campus and the fact that he is the only historian in the state ever to have a U.S. merchant marine vessel carry his name (the World War II Liberty ship the USS *George P. Garrison*). His classic 1903 book *Texas: A Contest of Civilizations* is blind to the historical role played by women. Garrison proved no exception to the trend of emphasizing the contributions of men to the development of the state. One would have to look far and wide to find women in the pages of academic histories written in the first half of the twentieth century by a panoply of great historians, including Charles W. Ramsdell, Eugene C. Barker, Walter Prescott Webb, and Rupert N. Richardson. For the most part, these historians studied institutional topics related to the political and economic history of the state. Women historians also began to appear on the academic scene during these years. Adele B. Looscan, Lilia M. Casis,

Julia Kathryn Garret, and Abigail Curlee Holbrook, to name a few, assumed leadership roles in the profession and in some cases published important academic studies, although they too generally gravitated toward institutional topics that at best paid little attention to women.

What few specialized studies of Texas women's history did appear prior to the mid-twentieth century considered almost exclusively those females who had historical purchase because they were related to men important in the state's past. These early studies generally treated women in one of two ways, focusing on women who were historical helpmates to men or on women who engaged in activities within a framework of patriarchy. Few, if any, of these academic historians considered women as independent historical persons in their own right in ways analogous to the treatment of the independent men who populate the pages of Texas academic history. This was certainly the case for a foundational book by Annie Doom Pickrell, *Pioneer Women in Texas*, published in 1929. Although a benchmark in historical writing about Texas women, this volume exclusively considered women within an explicit context of patriarchy. In the 475 pages of this book Pickrell presents four dozen biographies of Texas women, all of them married to prominent men and all referred to by the names of their husbands. Pickrell's volume, of course, represented the prevailing social and cultural conventions of its era regarding the place of women within the general standards of the times. Indeed, it would be unfair to criticize any early academic historian for reflecting unconsciously the values, ideals, and tenets of the times in which they wrote in characterizing Texas women. The purpose of academic history is not to reform and revamp social beliefs and moral principles in new ways different from the prevailing principles of earlier eras.

Nonetheless, as social values change, so too does written history in tandem because its fundamental purpose is to explain the evolution of a given society as it exists at the time the historian is working. As cultural conventions change, so too do the questions historians ask about the past. Academic history is thus as much about the beliefs of the present as it is about assessing the past as an atomized series of previous occurrences. It is therefore not surprising, starting in the mid-to-late twentieth century, that historians and others who wrote

about Texas began to focus their attention on women who had historical prominence outside the boundaries of patriarchy. In some cases,
this involved the recasting and reevaluation of women previously the
subject of patriarchal historical study. This literature harmonized with
the increasingly important role women began to play, not only in Texas
but also across the entire spectrum of American life. By the 1960s and
1970s, the growth in importance of women in all areas of society had
produced a blossoming of history about them. Women historians including A. Elizabeth Taylor, Sandra L. Meyers, and Ruthe Winegarten
began to publish important new studies based in the assumptions of an
independent, self-generated women's history which rapidly became a
professional subfield of US history by the 1970s, including in Texas.
The creation of professional women's history forums, the increased
prominence of women's history as seen in the pages of historical jour-
nals, and the creation of dedicated archival collections highlighting
women propelled this burgeoning historical literature into the main-
stream of academic writing about Texas history. In 1988, Anne Patton
Malone wrote a historiographical essay for a volume entitled *A Guide
to the History of Texas*. This essay marked the arrival of women's history
as an established frame of reference for the academic historical community in Texas.

Nonetheless, in spite of this new historiographical orientation, academic historians have faced a herculean task in integrating all aspects of
women's history into the story of Texas. This has been the case in part
because so much needed doing. Additionally, old icons and historical
memories fade away slowly because they have had long-standing tenure
in the traditional histories of the state, even in cases where important
academic studies have debunked previously held assumptions about the
role of women in Texas history. This has certainly been the case for the
history of Texas ranching and the cattle kingdom in the Lone Star State.
Few other topics in the state's history have been imbued with such ro-
manticism and popular interest than the story of the great ranches and
ranchers in Texas. From the nineteenth century to the twenty-first, this
topic has attracted the attention of novelists, nonfiction writers, and
historians, along with filmmakers and television producers, as a fruitful
area of interest. There is nothing more mythic to the ethos of Texas

than the image of the cowboy. Accordingly, academic historians have for several generations between writing good histories of the cattle frontier, the trail drives, the rise of the giant ranches of the state, and assessments of its fabled ranchers. As Jacqueline M. Moore has pointed out in her prizewinning 2010 book *Cow Boys and Cattle Men*, this has been predominately a masculine enterprise.

Women have largely been ancillary to this literature, with several notable studies by trend-setting historians. These include books by Joyce Gibson Roach, Sandra L. Meyers, Sara R. Massey, and several others. The volume now at hand dealing with Texas ranch women serves as welcome addition to these recent studies. It represents the research expertise of a group of historians who have spent years examining in detail a diverse array of specialized topics dealing with the history of ranch women in Texas. Their respective approaches range from considering women who led great ranches to those who barely eked an existence from small and precarious frontier holdings, and they include women from various ethnic backgrounds who found themselves working in the ranch country at levels from management to riding the range. Other essays in this volume consider women who competed in rodeos, an area not widely understood by the general public as a female domain. The essays that follow mostly represent papers presented at a symposium held at Midwestern State University (MSU) in Wichita Falls, Texas, June 2–3, 2016. The conference was organized by Leland Turner of the MSU History Department, with the assistance of Deborah Liles of the University of North Texas and Cecilia Gutierrez Venable of the University of Texas at El Paso. It brought together a group of historians, each of whom had long manifested an interest in the historical role women have played in the Texas cattle industry. Noted historian Caroline Castillo Crimm opened the symposium with a keynote address that surveyed the foundations of the cattle culture in Texas, with special attention given to noting how women as early as the Spanish colonial period participated in ways that proved historically significant. Ten additional historians thereafter presented their research and conclusions about a number of significant women who contributed to ranching during the past two centuries in Texas. "These were women who could ride and work cattle," Leland Turner noted about the subjects of these essays. "They were all living in a time and place when it was out of the ordinary to do what they did."

There is intentionality to all of the stories presented in this book. Granted, these ranch women came from varied backgrounds, personal circumstances, and economic and educational levels, and enjoyed different levels of success, but each of them nonetheless made her mark on history and, in so doing, greatly enriched the ranching heritage of Texas. Such is certainly the case for the Spanish colonial era. Amy Porter provides a solid overview of women in colonial Texas with reference to the ranching economy of the province, especially Maria Calvillo. Beyond those of the Spanish period, the women portrayed in this book fall into several categories. Several of them were elite leaders drawn from outstanding ranch families. As such they made a significant impact on their era as individuals with public recognition. They are for that reason among the best-known women whose lives are noted in the pages that follow. It is also likely that many readers of this volume will already be familiar with the general outlines of their careers. Alice East belonged to the family that owns and operates the San Antonio Viejo Ranch, which for a time was part of the famed King Ranch in South Texas. She and other women in the King family exercised significant influence on the development of ranching in the era as ranch managers. Cornelia Adair, born into an international family of singular wealth, divided her time between New York, Scotland, and the JA Ranch in North Texas. Her career was set squarely in the era when the vital center of the cattle industry shifted from smaller to gigantic cattle operations, a change she helped to bring about. Another South Texas woman noted in this book, Frances Kallison, also came from an important South Texas family with strong ties to the elite leaders of the San Antonio area. The Kallisons owned for several generations the preeminent farm and ranch store in the Alamo City. Frances's husband, Perry, was one of the best-known radio personalities in the region due to his early-morning agricultural radio show, which garnered a large following for several decades. Importantly, the Kallisons owned a ranch near San Antonio that eventually became a showplace. Like the King Ranch to the south of it, the Kallison operation attracted well-known and important visitors to Texas who desired to see ranch life in the state at close quarters. East, Adair, and Kallison were all women who had significant impact on their era, stemming from a combination of their own hard work and the standing of their families.

A second group of women whose lives are assessed in this volume is less well known to history and to the general public in Texas. Unlike the elite women noted above, the individuals in this group did not attain great wealth or have significant influence on the state because of their family connections. In some cases they came from relatively deprived economic backgrounds and never escaped that status. Nonetheless, they proved resourceful women, worked diligently in the ranch country, and represent unique individuals who survived by their own wits in the cattle country. Such was certainly the case for Lucinda Walker and other women of her place and time whose lives spanned the mid-nineteenth century and the era of the open range. Coming a bit later in that century, the Panhandle's Mary Jane Alexander constituted a historical model for an independent ranch woman whose creativity and initiative provided a steady but modest living for her family. Both are historical object lessons highlighting how independent, hardworking women could carve places for themselves in the patriarchal world of ranching prior to the twentieth century. Mable Doss and Mary Ketchum Meredith also fall into this category. Their activism in the fence-cutting wars has assured them a place in Texas ranch history. This is the case not because of their wealth and economic standing but because of their civic virtue and desire to bring order to a chaotic situation then plaguing the state. Mattie B. Morris Miller also falls into this category as a woman not well known to history, a woman who persevered. Inheriting a family ranch shared with her two brothers, she worked diligently during the early to mid-twentieth century to make the ranch prosper. It eventually did become a lucrative venture. Mattie became a social and economic leader in the region, something that resulted from her diligence.

A third category of women noted in this volume expands into an area that has not been much highlighted in the academic literature of Texas: women and rodeo. Other than stellar books by Joyce Gibson Roach and Sylvia Mahoney, little has been written about female rodeo in the state, an area mostly equated almost entirely with men. In this volume are the stories of two women who devoted their lives to rodeo, with both of them achieving success. It is likely that most people en-countering their stories will be doing so for the first time. Nonetheless, their careers constitute an important way that women have expanded the scope and impact of their presence in the ranching history of Texas.

All in all, the essays in this volume have the potential to accomplish several important goals. First, they document the lives of individual women important to Texas history, women who contributed to an ac-tivity that has traditionally been an all-male preserve in the historical literature. Second, these essays will undoubtedly point the way for additional studies of women and ranching and turn up stories that still cry out for recognition. In that regard, this book will have an impact larger than the ranching history of the state. There are women from all walks of life, across a large number of occupations and endeavors, whose contributions still need to be assessed by historians. Third, this book will demonstrate that there must be a new, all-encompassing con-ceptual dimension through which all academic historians of Texas on any subject should view women. All those who research and write Texas history should join in the common cause. No matter the topical focus, all must ask: How did what I am studying relate to women? Was there an identifiable female dimension to it? This book asks and answers those questions for the ranching history of Texas.

Chapter 1

Tejanas and Ranching
María Calvillo and Her Ranching Enterprises

Amy Porter

Texas ranching has long roots that reach to the colonial period. Early Spanish expeditions launched from Coahuila and Nuevo León provided the nucleus for future herds, as cattle lost or sometimes intentionally left behind bred successfully in the wild. Large feral herds eventually supplied one of the few economic opportunities for settlers moving north into Spanish Texas. Although men were expected to be the heads of household and publicly represent the family, especially the family businesses, women were also highly involved in such activities. María del Carmen Calvillo (1765–1856) is one of the women who stand out in the historical record.[1] She was remarkable in that she accumulated a large amount of land, oversaw huge ranching operations, and increased her business through periods of major political transition. Calvillo lived through the Spanish, Mexican, and Republic of Texas eras and into the US era of Texas history. While fortunes went up and down for many, Calvillo found ways to maintain and grow her holdings, at least until the last years of her life.

Calvillo has gained the attention of historians and the public due to high-profile events that impacted her family. An 1814 attack by Lipan Apaches on her father's ranch, the Rancho de las Cabras, (located in present-day Wilson County near Floresville) likely involved his own grandson. After this event, Spanish officials interviewed many witnesses and resultant documents, which still exist, provide critical insight into the happenings at the ranch. While Spanish authorities kept meticulous records of court cases and business transactions, paper was scarce and the literacy rate was fairly low on the frontier, meaning that letters and diaries from the time are uncommon and cannot be used to corroborate or expand on the events.[2]

While documentation of events in Calvillo's life and the success she had in ranching show her to be remarkable, her life experiences also show the possibilities for women under the Spanish legal system on the Texas frontier. Calvillo could own land because Spanish law allowed women to do so. Her husband participated in the independence movement and had to flee the San Antonio area, and the couple never reunited. Frontier Texas, though a rough place to live, provided opportunities for women to rise in society, which might not have been possible in more central parts of the Spanish empire.

The Calvillo story begins with the 1718 founding of the Mission San Antonio de Valero and the Presidio of San Antonio de Béxar. Presidial soldiers formed communities that often included their families. Two years later, Mission San José y San Miguel de Aguayo was built, followed by Missions San Juan Capistrano, San Francisco de la Espada, and Nuestra Señora de la Purísima Concepción de Acuña, which were first established in East Texas but moved to the San Antonio area in 1731. Missionaries' main goals were to Christianize and Hispanicize the diverse Indians of the region, focusing much of their daily schedule on instruction. Missions were intended to be nearly self-sufficient communities and used Indians to supplement labor shortages for agricultural, ranching, weaving, and other necessary tasks that benefited the mission economy. As a result of their early arrival in the area and their need to feed their occupants, the missions were granted vast ranch lands that later settlers would covet.[3]

In 1731, Spain brought fifteen Canary Island families to help populate the northern frontier of New Spain, as Spain had difficulty convincing people to move to its northern frontier where conditions were challenging.[4] These Canary Islanders formed the Villa de San Fernando de Béxar, received valuable parcels of land, and founded the local *cabildo*, a type of city council. Béxar suffered as a result of being a great distance from other markets, and it experienced raids by Lipan Apaches, Comanches, and other Indian peoples.[5] Persistent epidemic disease resulted in high infant and child mortality rates and a life expectancy in the San Antonio area hovering around age thirty-two for much of the Spanish colonial period. Dangerous work in the military and a pattern of older men marrying younger women meant that widowhood was common in the settlement. Census documents from the colonial era show numerous households headed by women. Examining wills show that many women who had been widowed remarried, sometimes more than once. The many widows of San Antonio meant, given Spanish property law, that some women would become important landowners and ranchers.[6]

Ranching during the colonial era was not as it is today. Without fences, ranching required rounding up wild cattle rather than tending to corralled livestock daily. As historian Jesús F. de la Teja wrote, the common use of the term *rancho* in Texas points to the small pieces of land that Bexareños used to ranch in the San Antonio area, unlike the larger haciendas that existed to the south in Mexico. The missions had massive ranch lands, but individual citizens who became involved in ranching tended to have smaller landholdings. One contentious issue with ranching during this period had to do with branding cattle. Missions and individuals used brands, but there were large numbers of unclaimed and unbranded cattle. After the Spanish Crown claimed these in 1778, the new, highly contested Spanish law then required a fee or fine for the killing of unbranded cattle. Some ranches in the San Antonio area also raised goats and sheep, known as *ganado menor*. The Calvillo family's Rancho de las Cabras, though involved in the ranching of many different animals, raised goats, as the name suggests, and sheep.[7]

In 1760, María Calvillo's father, Ignacio Calvillo, married Doña María Antonia de Arocha, who came from an important ranching and Canary Islander family. Together they had five or six children, of whom María would be the oldest surviving child.[8] Ignacio Calvillo first leased and then owned a small ranch known as El Paso de los Mujeres (near their future Rancho de las Cabras), which a 1786 report noted had sixty livestock total, thirty of which were branded.[9] His ranching efforts would not remain small-scale, however, and, as his ranching enterprises grew, Calvillo requested permission to drive cattle to another market with his brothers-in-law Juan and Ignacio de Arocha.[10] It is unclear exactly when Calvillo increased his holdings to include much of the Rancho de las Cabras, but one source indicates that he filed for the title in 1809. Certainly Calvillo had been ranching (likely leasing land from Mission Espada) in the vicinity of Las Cabras, if not on part of it, by the late 1780s.[11] Calvillo became an important rancher in the area, and his ties to the Arocha family as well as his daughter María's marriage to a member of another ranching family, the Delgados, likely helped his ranching. To better understand the transition of ownership from Ignacio Calvillo to his daughter María due to an attack on the ranch, archival evidence must be analyzed.

When María was in her mid to late forties, various attempts to make Mexico independent of Spain played out on the far northern frontier, with resultant turmoil and suffering. After Father Miguel Hidalgo y Costilla called for Mexican independence with his Grito de Dolores speech on September 16, 1810, people began to choose sides. A failed *independentista* uprising known as the Casas Revolt took place in San Antonio in 1811, foreshadowing the fighting that would continue over the next few years. The next major upheaval came with the joint Mexican-US Gutiérrez-Magee Expedition and its clash with the troops of Spanish general Joaquín de Arredondo. On August 18, 1813, Arredondo's troops crushed the Republican Army of the North—the troops of the Gutiérrez-Magee Expedition—approximately twenty miles south of San Antonio at the Battle of Medina. Out of fourteen hundred members of the Republican Army of the North, over thirteen hundred died. Arredondo imprisoned widows of the participants, holding them in a house he called La Quinta, where they faced sexual assault and endless labor. To punish those who did not oppose the rebellion, Arredondo took away land, affecting women as well as men; he also ordered that households not have guns and required farmers and ranchers join a militia to protect the community from rebels. The result was land loss, agricultural production decline and lack of food, and increased Indian attacks, especially on the ranches farthest from town.[12]

In this atmosphere, an Indian attack at the Rancho de las Cabras was no surprise. In 1814, a raid by Lipan Apaches resulted in the death of Ignacio Calvillo, María's father. Spanish authorities interviewed the many people who were at the ranch, and the investigations uncovered the possibility that María's nephew Ignacio Casanova had been involved in the attack. As a result of the death of her father, María inherited the ranch and some other property.[13]

This story highlights several important points. For one, María, like many women of this time, gained property through inheritance. Second, scholars know more about María Calvillo and the ranch due to this event and the numerous related documents created by the Spanish officials. Third, the interviews show the size of the ranch and impart the idea that this was a small community rather than a ranch that was home to only one family. There were many people living and working on the ranch at the time of the attack: Ignacio Calvillo and his wife (Doña María), two of their daughters, María and Juana, and Juana's husband, José Saucedo, and their children. Additionally, there was a doctor, at least two servants (as Ignacio and María each had one), eight laborers, a shepherd, and a tailor.[14] While not the largest ranch in the San Antonio area, the number of people at the ranch at the time of the attack show it to be significant in its operations, especially during a time when many Bexareños were not staying out on the outlying ranches due to increased Indian attacks. This horrible event changed María's life as she transitioned into a large landowner with the assistance of Spanish laws that allowed her to inherit her father's property.[15]

Spanish law required that all children inherit property fairly equally, so daughters inherited land just as sons did. Thus, women were landowners. They signed contracts; they bought, sold, inherited, and willed land; and they sued over property in courts. While these laws allowed women to own and manage property, men—generally husbands (widows often remarried) but sometimes other male relatives—often represented women in courts or in business matters. Despite the implications of these laws for women's economic influence, the social expectations for women in Spanish San Antonio contradicted their legal power in some ways. The ideal woman was to be pure, loyal, religious, and stay out of public as much as possible. Yet Spanish women on the

frontier of New Spain in the San Antonio area helped in their husbands' or families' shops and ran the businesses when their husbands
traveled. The same was true of running ranches. Women managed
ranches when their husbands traveled and after they died.[16] These laws
and customs allowed María Calvillo to run the Rancho de las Cabras.

María Calvillo's life can only be understood based on the documentation available. Due to the attack on the ranch and her large landholdings, she appears in the historical record more than many other women
of the period. Despite these official documents, historians lack diaries,
letters, and personal sources that might help us understand more about
her life experiences and thoughts.

Even before the attack on the ranch, María appears in a fascinating
document in the Bexar Archives. This document, dated 1806, granted
María Calvillo power of attorney for Antonio Baca in order to collect some debts for him in Nacogdoches. The document specifically
mentions a twenty-one-peso debt from one man and a twenty-two-
peso debt from another man.[17] There is no explanation as to why Baca
chose Calvillo to collect his debts or why she might have been traveling to Nacogdoches, but it might be related to the fact that her father
did some business there on occasion or that she was traveling with her
husband. What is so remarkable about this document is that women
were much more likely to give men power of attorney than vice versa,
as women were often represented in public by men. This document
reveals that María had business or legal experience before she owned
the Rancho de las Cabras. This served her well once she became a
prominent rancher.[18]

María married Gavino Delgado (Juan Gavino de la Trinidad Delgado), a man from another important ranching family, in 1781. It appears
that they initially lived on her father's *solar*, a lot in the town along San
Pedro Creek, and later moved into a house at Mission San Juan around
1810. María received title for this land in 1823. María and Gavino had
several children together, but the children possibly died at a young
age. In her 1856 will affidavit, María named two adopted children as
her heirs. The origins of these adopted children are unclear, but it was
common in this time for families to adopt children due to the high
mortality rates in the area. Some adoptees were relatives, godchildren,

or neighbors. In such a manner, a frontier community could absorb orphans and provide some stability.[19]

Another person in María's home may have been an Indian. A baptismal record from 1796 notes that Gavino Delgado rescued a one-year-old Comanche girl, named María Concepción, who had been a captive of the Apaches. There is no mention of María Calvillo in this document, and the records do not say what happened to María Concepción, so it is not clear if she stayed in the Calvillo household. There was an active captive trade on the southern plains, and Spanish citizens paid ransoms known as *rescates* to rescue captives. Spanish citizens raised these Indians, primarily women and children, and taught them Christianity and Spanish ways. The roles of these Indians, often called *criados*, ranged from servants to adopted family members. This practice was quite common in New Mexico, but it was also present in the San Antonio area, and it appears that such an experience touched the Calvillo household.[20]

As previously mentioned, María's husband participated in early attempts for independence and fled the area for a period of time. In his writings concerning the 1811 independence actions, José Antonio Navarro noted that Gavino Delgado, Francisco Travieso, and Vicente Flores joined Juan Bautista Casas and troops who marched into main plaza in the villa of San Fernando de Béxar to represent residents' support for independence. Such public displays of support were problematic when royalists quickly retook control of Béxar. Delgado's absence and separation from María possibly helped her in 1813 and just after when General Arredondo imprisoned women and confiscated property from those who did not try to stop the rebellion. Documents make no mention of María's political ideas, but a separation from her husband might have been the only thing that prevented authorities from assuming they held similar ideas. It is also possible that her father served as protection for her in this era of fights for independence (at least until his death in 1814), although his political beliefs are unclear.[21]

Sometime after the separation, María began to refer to herself as a widow, although Delgado did not die until 1825 in Béxar.[22] Though this situation may sound unusual, divorce was likely not a possibility

for María. One historian noted that divorce was very uncommon in
Spanish Texas. In fact, in extreme cases of abuse or abandonment, the
Catholic Church would try to reconcile the couple; if no reconciliation
was possible, only then could the couple separate. Neither party could
remarry until one died. No such church proceedings have been found
in María's case, but the laws and customs meant that divorce was not
really an option.[23]

As a widow, María continued to manage her ranch. Though there
are not records that detail inventories of livestock on María's ranch, an
1817 document lists "Doña María Calvillo" as one of thirty-six Bexareños who owned livestock that included cattle, horses, mules, and
sheep; the list omitted citizens who owned small numbers of animals.[24]
Despite a lack of livestock numbers, there is physical evidence of María
Calvillo's ranching activities. Nora Ríos McMillan writes that archaeological evidence points to the fact that the Calvillo ranches "prospered under her direction. . . . Her workforce became indispensable
in constructing and repairing wooden picket fences, tending to livestock—taking care of newborns, feeding the stock during droughts,
branding and exporting—as well as guarding against cattle rustling.[25]
In the 1820s, María appears in the historical record as she requested
replacement land titles for titles that had been lost or stolen in the 1814
attack on Las Cabras ranch, and she petitioned for property lost in the
fights for independence. In 1834, she filed a petition for a title to land
along the San Antonio River. Calvillo performed due diligence in at-
taining titles to her lands and in requesting more land. The 1840s did
see a change for Calvillo as she sold some of her Las Cabras lands to
Edward Dwyer in 1845. It is unclear why María sold this land, though
it is possible that in her advanced age the lands were too much for her
to administer.[26]

In the last years of her life, María entered the public records again as
community members and neighbors questioned her ability to run her
own affairs. In 1851, Lucas Muñoz, a guardian to her adopted son Antonio Durán, filed a lawsuit to declare María del Carmen Calvillo *non
compos mentis*, or not of sound mind, due to her age. A jury heard this
case, and lawyers including Ángel Navarro questioned at least twelve
male witnesses. The jury found Calvillo "*non compos mentis*, and from

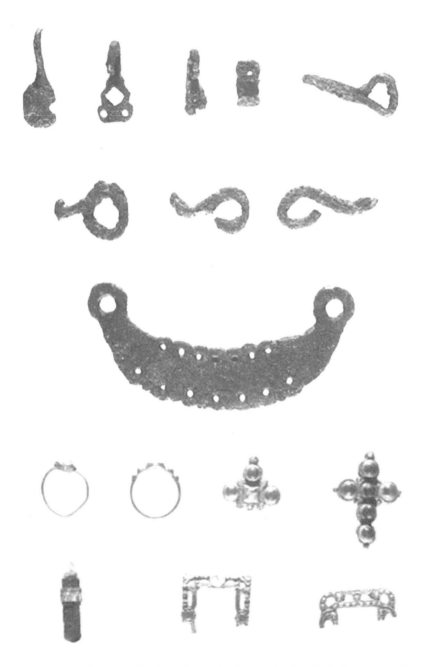

Figure 1. Artifacts found at Rancho de las Cabras in the 1970s (see note 11). Courtesy of University of Texas at San Antonio, Center for Archaeological Research, and San Antonio Missions National Historic Park, National Park Service.

her extreme old age entirely incapable of managing her own business-es." The court named Muñoz as guardian of her estate.[27]

After María died in 1856, legal problems began with her estate. Inés Calvillo de la Garza, her niece, filed a document claiming that María had died intestate, and Inés was named the administrator of her es-tate. Then Antonio Durán filed suit against Inés, claiming that María Calvillo had a will, and he challenged the role of Inés. The court brought in several witnesses to provide testimony about María's will. As such, the court reconstructed the Calvillo will, which then named María Concepción Gortarí and Antonio Durán, her adopted children, as María's heirs who would share in her property equally. The recon-structed will named Muñoz as the guardian and executor of the estate, and the court revoked Inés's position.[28] One odd issue was that an af-fidavit of María Calvillo's will was filed with Bexar County in 1851, which noted that she had made a will in 1845. This document named both Gortarí and Durán as her only heirs and described her property as her stone house at Mission San Juan, irrigation rights, half a *suerte* of land, and the pasturage that she owned. She also declared that she had some livestock, although she did not note exact numbers. This document had witnesses who saw her make her mark and noted her "inability to write." The affidavit was recorded in Spanish, unlike the other documents related to her estate around this time, and it was filed the same month as her *non compos mentis* case.[29] If this document was accurate, then the court upheld her wishes to name Gortarí and Durán as her heirs.

One major question is just how common or uncommon were María Calvillo's experiences. Certainly much of her success in managing her ranch and expanding her landholdings was due to her own resolve. Yet there were other women who played major roles in ranching in Span-ish Texas. For example, in San Antonio in the late 1770s, the second largest cattle owner was María Ana Curbelo, who owned Rancho Las Mulas. Another woman, Leonor Delgado, ranked fifth at the same time.[30] Rosa María Hinojosa de Ballí owned a huge amount of land in what would become South Texas and South Padre Island. Ballí was born in 1752, and at her death in 1803 she had over a million acres of land in present-day South Texas and northern Mexico (Tamaulipas).

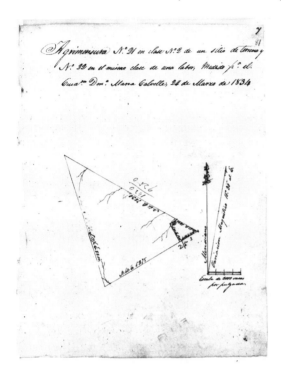

Figure 2. A portion of the deed for Maria Calvillo's land, signed by Juan Seguín, March 24, 1834. Courtesy of the Texas Government Land Office.

She inherited some land when her husband died but greatly increased her property through many business deals and land grants.[31]

There were many other women who had smaller ranches. For example, in her 1785 will, Juana de Hollos claimed part of the San Bartolomé Ranch that she and her deceased husband had acquired during their marriage. She also owned a cattle brand and claimed the cattle on her ranch and in a summer pasture in town.[32] In María Feliciana Durán's 1814 will, she explained that she owned two leagues of ranchland and had cattle with her own brand. She also noted that she had lost many cattle due to the attacks of rebels and Indians during the independence fights and ensuing increased Indian raids of the 1810s.[33]

Women generally acquired land through inheritance, but as widows many were able to acquire more land through grants or purchases. An 1812 document in the Bexar Archives that names the *síndicos* of the ranches—officials who oversaw the slaughter, sale, and regulations concerning livestock—listed the Béxar area ranches and owners. The list notes forty-three ranchers, including three women. Other documents that note brands for the San Antonio area show a larger number of women ranchers with brands, including María Josefa de la Garza, who had three different brands, and Gertrudes Ureña, who had six different brands.[34] Thus, it appears that while it was much more common for men to be involved in ranching than women, women ranchers were not uncommon.

María Calvillo played an important role in the development of the Rancho de las Cabras, but she was one of many women ranchers in the Spanish colonial period. In some ways what is most remarkable is that Calvillo held onto her land when there was a great deal of Tejano land loss, especially in the San Antonio area. While historians have made a strong case that Tejanos are at the roots of Texas ranching, the narrative should be expanded to include Tejanas, as the likes of Calvillo played significant roles as early Texas ranchers.[35]

After Calvillo's death, the Rancho de las Cabras continued to be important. When Edward Dwyer bought the land in the 1840s, he was the mayor of San Antonio. After Dwyer died, his wife, Mariana Leal Dwyer, a Canary Island descendant, inherited her share of the ranch, which she held until her death in 1867, when her portion then passed on to her son Joseph Dwyer. The Rancho de las Cabras changed ownership thirteen times after the death of Edward Dwyer until the State of Texas acquired it in 1982, and then in 1995 the land became part of the National Park Service.[36]

Today park rangers take visitors to the Rancho de las Cabras site several times a year and explain the rich history of the ranch and the archaeological work that has been conducted on the site. With the designation of the San Antonio missions as a UNESCO World Heritage site in 2015, the Rancho de las Cabras may well receive more visitors and gain more attention. This in turn means that the story of María Calvillo and Tejana ranchers in general will likely become better known by locals and tourists alike who are seeking more information about the history of Texas. As an archaeologist who worked on the Rancho de las Cabras site wrote, "The potential for Rancho de las Cabras is very great. Rancho de las Cabras is one of the best preserved colonial sites in Texas in terms of archaeology, and it is certainly one of the most important in terms of cultural and historical studies. It would not be excessive to say that it is a site which is critical to our understanding of the development of the San Antonio River valley."[37] This understanding rests upon the significance of ranching in the history of early Texas. And within the story of ranching in San Antonio, María Calvillo and other women ranchers play a crucial role.

Notes

1. Jesús F. de la Teja, *San Antonio de Béxar: A Community on New Spain's Northern Frontier* (Albuquerque: University of New Mexico Press, 1995), 115.

2. For attempts to establish schools that would have increased literacy, see Donald E. Chipman, *Spanish Texas, 1519–1821* (Austin: University of Texas Press, 1992), 256–57. Book ownership was fairly low as well. See Amy M. Porter, *Their Lives, Their Wills: Women in the Spanish Borderlands, 1750–1846* (Lubbock: Texas Tech University Press, 2015), 45–46. Most testators in San Antonio in the late Spanish colonial period could not sign wills. See Porter, *Their Lives, Their Wills*, 45–46, 118–20.

3. Teja, *San Antonio de Béxar*, 8–9; Gilberto M. Hinojosa, "The Religious-Indian Communities: The Goals of the Friars," in *Tejano Origins of Eighteenth-Century San Antonio*, ed. Gerald E. Poyo and Gilberto M. Hinojosa (Austin: University of Texas Press, 1991), 61–83.

4. Teja, *San Antonio de Béxar*, 18.

5. Ibid., 8–9, 100–101.

6. Alicia Vidaurreta Tjarks, "Comparative Demographic Analysis of Texas, 1777–1793," in *New Spain's Far Northern Frontier: Essays on Spain in the American West, 1540–1821*, ed. David J. Weber (Albuquerque: University of New Mexico Press, 1979), 149, 159; Elizabeth A. Fenn, *Pox Americana: The Great Smallpox Epidemic of 1775–82* (New York: Hill and Wang, 2001), 6, 15, 43, 138, 146, 157, 209–12; Oakah L. Jones Jr., *Los Paisanos: Spanish Settlers on the Northern Frontier of New Spain* (Norman: University of Oklahoma Press, 1979), 140; Porter, *Their Lives, Their Wills*, 21–22.

7. Jack Jackson, *Los Mesteños: Spanish Ranching in Texas, 1721–1821* (College Station: Texas A&M University Press, 1986), 9–11, 126–27, 155–56, 224–25; Teja, *San Antonio de Béxar*, 97–112.

8. Sources vary on the number of children that the Calvillos had. Calvillo's wife, Antonia de Arocha, came from Canary Island families on both her father and mother's side. Nora Ríos McMillan, "A Woman of Worth: Ana María del Carmen Calvillo," in *Tejano Epic: Essays in Honor of Félix D. Almaráz, Jr.*, ed. Arnoldo De León (Austin: Texas State Historical Association, 2005), 34; Donald E. Chipman and Harriett Denise Joseph, *Notable Men and Women of Spanish Texas* (Austin: University of Texas Press, 1999), 274; Jackson, *Los Mesteños*, 71–72. For María Calvillo's baptismal record, see "Calvillo, María del Carmen," in *San Fernando Church Confirmations, 1759, and Baptismals, Book I, 1731–1775*, compiled by John Ogden Leal (San Antonio, 1976), 9 (viewed in the Texana Room at the San Antonio Public Library).

9. Jackson, *Los Mesteños*, 230.

10. Cattle were generally driven to Coahuila but sometimes to East Texas or Louisiana. Jackson, *Los Mesteños*, 309–10.

11. Ibid., 413–14. It is important to note that the Rancho de las Cabras began as pastureland for Mission Espada. Examining the various reports of Spanish officials, one scholar estimates that Mission Espada had 733 horses, 2,621 sheep, and 3,000 cattle, as well as some oxen, mules, donkeys, pigs, and goats. These numbers indicate major livestock holdings, although many claimed by the mission were likely unbranded. In addition, many archaeological excavations by the University of Texas at San Antonio's Center for Archaeological Research have been conducted at the Rancho de las Cabras, providing a wealth of information about the historic site. Most of the archaeological work focused on the mid-1700s to the early 1800s. Archaeologists have pieced together maps of a compound that had walls, several rooms, a chapel, and defensive bastions that were apparently added later. Metal objects including hand-forged nails, rings, crucifixes, kitchen items, glass bottles, pottery shards, and other items were also found. While most of the pottery was locally made, some came from Puebla and Michoacan in Mexico, and some porcelain even came from China. The archaeological reports indicate that such items were common at San Antonio missions and also indicate the extent of trade networks within the Spanish empire. For more on the history of the site, see James E. Ivey, *Archaeological Testing at Rancho de las Cabras, 41WN30, Wilson County, Texas, Second Season* (San Antonio: University of Texas at San Antonio, Center for Archaeological Research, 1983), 16, 20, 23, 28; Anne A. Fox and Brett A. Houk, *Archaeological and Historical Investigations at Rancho de las Cabras, 41WN30, Wilson County, Texas, Fourth Season* (San Antonio: University of Texas at San Antonio, Center for Archaeological Research, 1998), 3, 20, 24.

12. Chipman, *Spanish Texas*, 232–37; Bradley Folsom, *Arredondo: Last Spanish Ruler of Texas and Northeastern New Spain* (Norman: University of Oklahoma Press, 2017), 70–71, 88–92, 96–98, 103–4.

13. *Sumaria* against Residents of Calvillo Ranch for His Murder (April 15, 1814), Bexar Archives, Texana Room, San Antonio Public Library, roll 053: 713–14, 728.

14. Ibid.

15. Under Spanish law, María and other women had fairly strong property rights. Women often brought property into their marriages as it would remain theirs. Some wealthier women had dowries, and while the dowry was a gift to the newlyweds, the husband could not sell the property without his wife's consent. In addition, Spain had community property laws that allowed married couples to share equally in all property gained in a marriage. Women could and did inherit property. See Porter, *Their Lives, Their Wills*, 7.

16. Chipman and Joseph, *Notable Men and Women of Spanish Texas*, 265; Porter, *Their Lives, Their Wills*, 7–8. See also Jean A. Stuntz, *Hers, His, and Theirs: Community Property Law in Spain and Early Texas* (Lubbock: Texas Tech University Press, 2010, 2005), 25–27, 72, 77.

17. "Power of Attorney from Antonio Baca to collect debts at Nacogdoches," SF, 5/6/1806, Bexar Archives, roll 034: 0632–33.

18. Jean A. Stuntz notes how women often gave men power of attorney. See Stuntz, *Hers, His, and Theirs*, 72–73.

19. Ríos McMillan, "Woman of Worth," 31–32. For other examples of orphans in wills, see the will of María Concepción de Estrada, Spanish Archives of Bexar County (hereafter SABC), WE 36, 11/2/1815, and the will of Julián de Arocha, SABC, WE 5, 6/28/1811. Ivey, *Archaeological Testing at Rancho de las Cabras*, 33. Nora Ríos McMillan suggests that Antonio Dúran might be an illegitimate (natural) child of María's brother Francisco Calvillo. Ríos McMillan also noted that María Calvillo named a guardian, Lucas Muñoz, for Durán in her will, so due to María's age at the time, and the fact that Durán was a minor, he could not have been an illegitimate child of María. See Ríos McMillan, "Woman of Worth," 38. Another researcher, Robert García, suggests that Antonio Durán might have been an illegitimate child of Lucas Muñoz, who was later named as a guardian. García found that an 1833 baptismal record for José Antonio Jesús Muños named Lucas Muños as the father, naming Durán as a natural child (illegitimate). The mother, Josefa Jaime, was the common-law wife of Blas Durán. Josefa Jaime had another child, named María Concepción. In addition, an 1850 census of Bexar County lists "Maria Calvea" living in a household with "Antonio Muños," who is possibly this Antonio Durán. Robert Garcia, "María del Carmen Calvillo de Delgado and Her Two Adopted Children," unpublished paper, September 28, 2003, 1–4. Thus, researchers have theories as to the connections between Calvillo and her two adopted children and the guardian Lucas Muñoz, but they cannot be proven.

20. "María de la Concepción," in *San Fernando Church Baptismals, 1793–1812* compiled by John Ogden Leal (San Antonio, 1976), 23 (viewed in the Texana Room at the San Antonio Public Library). For more information on *rescate* and *criados*, see David J. Weber, *The Spanish Frontier in North America* (New Haven: Yale University Press, 1994), 126–27; James F. Brooks, *Captives and Cousins: Slavery, Kinship, and Community in the Southwest Borderlands* (Chapel Hill: University of North Carolina Press, 2002), 18, 30, 33, 50, 123, 127, 147; Pekka Hämäläinen, *The Comanche Empire* (New Haven: Yale University Press), 26, 84, 250–53; and Julianna Barr, *Peace Came in the Form of a Woman: Indians and Spaniards in the Texas Borderlands* (Chapel Hill: University of North Carolina Press, 2007), 164–70. María Concepción Gortarí was named as an heir in María Calvillo's will, but I have not found documents showing that the Apache María Concepción was the same person as María Concepción Gortarí.

21. Ríos McMillan, "Woman of Worth," 31–32; José Antonio Navarro, *Defending Mexican Valor in Texas: José Antonio Navarro's Historical Writings, 1852–1857*, ed. David R. McDonald and Timothy M. Matovina (Abilene: State House Press, 1995), 67–68.

22. Ríos McMillan, "Woman of Worth," 31–32.

23. Light Townsend Cummins, "Church Courts, Marriage Breakdown, and Separation in Spanish Louisiana, West Florida, and Texas, 1763–1836," *Journal*

of Texas Catholic History and Culture 4 (1993): 100–102, 109, 111–12.

24. Jackson, *Los Mesteños*, 637.

25. Ríos McMillan, "Woman of Worth," 35–36.

26. "Petitions for Return of Property Lost during the Anglo-American Invasion, San Juan Capistrano," November 14, 1818, Bexar Archives, M, roll 062: 0341–45; "Land Petitions Filed by Her, Ana María Arocha, and others," BX, roll 117: 0266–73, October 14, 1828; "Search for Her and Juan Montes' Land Titles," BX roll 146: 0209–18, November 23, 1831; "Titulo de Posesión," María Calvillo, Texas GLO, Abstract 5, File # SC000120: 4, Wilson County, accessed July 18, 2017, www.glo.texas.gov/; Fox and Houk, *Archaeological and Historical Investigations*, 30; Rosalind Z. Rock, "Rancho de las Cabras: A Spanish Colonial Mission Ranch Offers Partnership Opportunities," *Cultural Resource Management (CRM)*, no. 11 (1997): 32.

27. María del Carmen Calvillo *Non Compos Mentis* Case, Bexar County Clerk Records, AB 581, 56, 1851, viewed in SABC.

28. "Estate of María del Carmen Calvillo, deceased. Petition of Ynez Calvillo y Garza," Bexar County Clerk Records, C 533, 56, 1856, SABC; "Petition of Antonio Durán et al. for the Probate of the Last Will and Testament of María del Carmen Calvillo," Bexar County Clerk Records, C 488, 530/533, 1856, SABC.

29. María del Carmen Calvillo to Ma. C. Gortarí Durán, Bexar County Clerk Records, J1, 68, 1851, SABC. A *suerte* is a piece of land generally used for agriculture. The document says "*la mitad del ganado que actualmente poseo*," which translates to "the half of the livestock that I now own." There appear to be no inventories of estates for Ignacio Calvillo or María Calvillo, so numbers of livestock owned are not known.

30. Chipman and Joseph, *Notable Men and Women of Spanish Texas*, 274.

31. Clotilde P. García, "Hinojosa De Balli, Rosa Maria," *Handbook of Texas Online*, accessed July 13, 2017, http: //www.tshaonline.org/handbook/online/articles/fhi50; Ríos-McMillan, "Woman of Worth," 30.

32. The Last Will and Testament of Juana de Hollos, August 13, 1785, SABC, WE 60.

33. The Last Will and Testament of María Feliciana Durán, WE 29, June 25, 1814, SABC.

34. Jackson, *Los Mesteños*, 511–13, 634, 649–51.

35. For the importance of early Tejano ranching, see Teja, *San Antonio de Béxar*; Andrés Tijerina, *Tejano Empire: Life on the South Texas Ranchos* (College Station: Texas A&M University Press, 1998); and Jackson, *Los Mesteños*.

36. Oculus, *Rancho de Los Cabras Cultural Landscape Report*, prepared for the U. S. Department of the Interior, National Park Service, San Antonio Missions National Historical Park, Intermountain Region (1998), 1-19, 2-45–46, accessed July 29, 2017, https: //www.nps.gov/saan/getinvolved/upload/Rancho-CLR-November-1998_Reduced.pdf.

37. Ivey, *Archaeological Testing at Rancho de las Cabras*, 42.

Chapter 2

In Search of Lucinda

Women in the Cattle Industry in Early Texas

Deborah M. Liles

Listed among the names of providers of beef for the Confederate Army in 1862 is one Lucinda Walker, one of the countless women whose participation in the cattle industry has been overlooked, forgotten, or hardly noticed. No conclusive information about her has been found other than that on November 1 and November 20, 1862, after the Confederate draft took men by the thousands away from their homes, farms, and ranches, Lucinda sold a total of 983 pounds of beef for $49.15 to First Lieutenant J. T. Rowland at Red River Station, Montague County, Texas.[1]

Lucinda Walker represents the many women involved in the livestock industry before 1866 and symbolizes the various roadblocks researchers confront when reconstructing women's lives and participation in early livestock economics. She cannot be located on any local tax records under her own name. Several census records render possibilities, including a thirty-two-year-old L. Walker in Parker County, a thirty-nine-year-old Lucinda Walker in Polk County, a twenty-nine-year-old Lucinda Walker in Hunt County, and a thirty-nine-year-old Lucinda Walker in Ouachita County, Arkansas. Because the distance between Polk, Hunt, and Ouachita Counties and the Red River Station would make the sale of two small-to-medium-sized beef cows prohib-

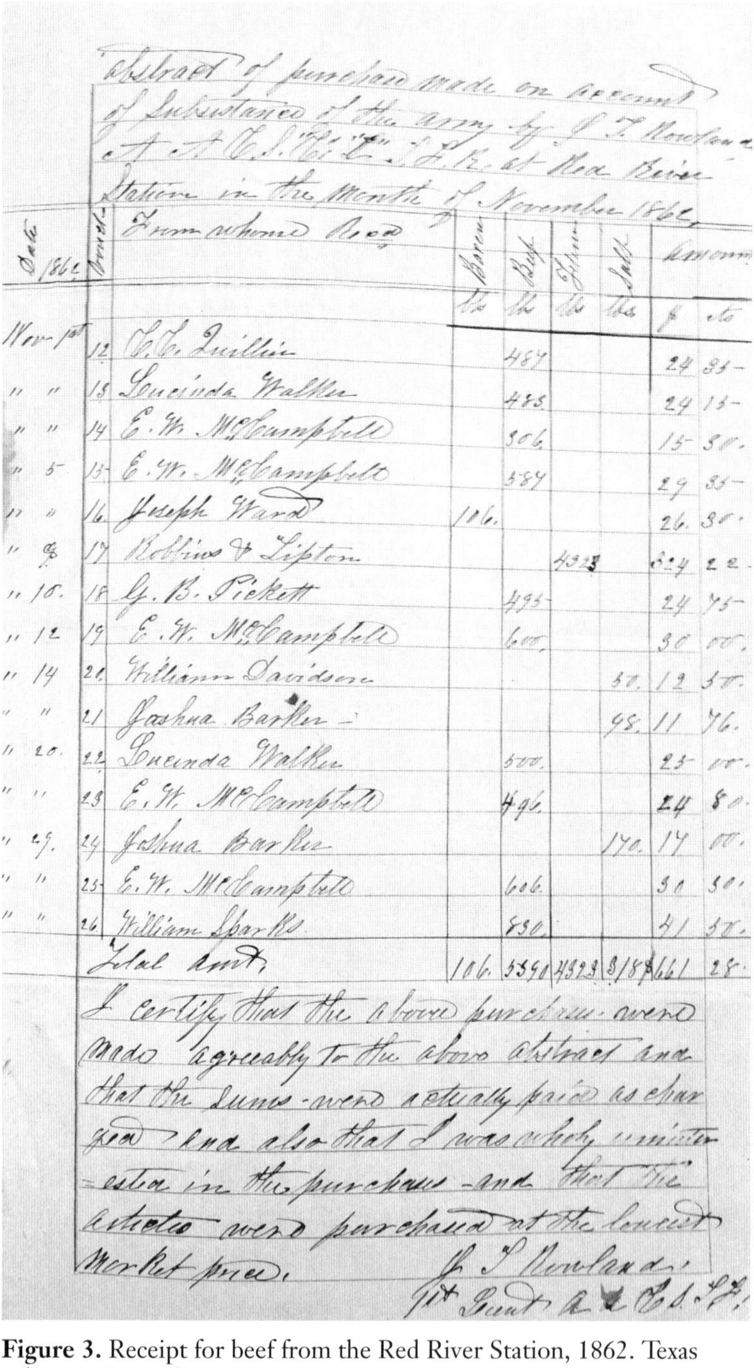

Abstract of purchase made on account of Subsistance of the army by J. T. Rowland A. A. C. S. at Red River Station in the Month of November 1862

Date 1862	Voucher	From whom Recd	Bacon lbs	Beef lbs	Flour lbs	Salt lbs	Amount $	cts
Nov 1st	12	C. C. Quillin		487			24	35
" "	13	Lucinda Walker		483			24	15
" "	14	E. W. McCampbell		306			15	30
" 5	15	E. W. McCampbell		587			29	35
" "	16	Joseph Ward	106.				26.	50
" 8	17	Robbins & Lipton			4323		324	22
" 10	18	G. B. Pickett		495			24	75
" 12	19	E. W. McCampbell		600.			30	00
" 14	20	William Davidson				50.	12	50
" "	21	Joshua Barker				48.	11	76
" 20	22	Lucinda Walker		500.			25	00
" "	23	E. W. McCampbell		496.			24	80
" 29	24	Joshua Barker				170.	17	00
" "	25	E. W. McCampbell		606.			30	30
" "	26	William Sparks		830.			41	50
		Total Amt	106.	5590	4323	318	661	28

I certify that the above purchases were made agreeably to the above abstract and that the sums were actually paid as charged and also that I was wholly uninterested in the purchase and that the articles were purchased at the lowest market price.

J. T. Rowland
1st Lieut A. A. C. S.

Figure 3. Receipt for beef from the Red River Station, 1862. Texas Adjutant General's Department, Texas State Archives Commission.

itive, it is probable that none of these is the same Lucinda. It is more conceivable that she was residing in Parker County, and she may have been related to Felix Walker, a soldier at the Red River Station, but there is nothing to support this supposition.[2]

At this point the question becomes why does she even matter? Her two cows represent such a miniscule amount in the overall number of cattle procured by Texas quartermasters during the war years, much less in the larger history of ranching in the state, making her inclusion seem futile. She matters for multiple reasons, and one is that by selling beef, Walker, like many other women, participated in the livestock economy before the observed great era of cattle trailing began in 1866. Additionally, while the sum of $49.15 may appear to be a negligible amount, a different perspective materializes when one takes into consideration that a private in Confederate service was paid $12 a month, making the beef money more than four month's pay.[3]

The search for Lucinda Walker has produced more questions than answers, but it has also led to the discovery of other women engaged in the livestock trade before the end of the Civil War. Much as with Lucinda, there are so few records for many of the women that their participation can easily be missed. A brief survey of county-level sources, the 1860 census, and local tax records renders evidence that women of all ages and various ethnicities participated in the early livestock business.[4]

In Atascosa County, located in South Texas, ten women identified as stock raisers are listed in the 1860 census records. They ranged in age from twenty-eight to sixty-one, and each was either head of household or lived where another woman was listed as household head. Margaret Brown, head of household and stock raiser, was fifty-one and from North Carolina. She resided with a twenty-year-old male, also a stock raiser, an eighteen-year-old male, and a fourteen-year-old female, undoubtedly adding to Margaret's responsibilities. Margaret declared $280 worth of livestock in the 1859 property taxes but did not report in 1860, creating another broken trail. There is, however, a Rachel Brown, who declared six horses worth $200, 280 head of cattle worth $1,680, and $600 in miscellaneous property. Rachel Brown's taxes from the preceding year show that she had four horses worth $160,

170 head of cattle worth $1,020, one hundred hogs, and seventeen oxen. Her livestock increase within a year, 33 percent in horses and 39 percent in cattle, represents a significant and noteworthy gain in her stock holdings and its value during the prewar years. Rachel Brown is not listed as a stock raiser on the census—there is only a blank space for her profession—but Rachel's husband is so listed despite the fact that he did not declare any livestock in his 1859 and 1860 property taxes. The cases of Margaret Brown and Rachel Brown demonstrate the sporadic nature of records and how professional allocations in the census records remove women from ranching studies by shifting the focus to their husbands.[5]

Another Atascosa County stock raiser was forty-seven-year-old Mississippian Mary G. Mills. In 1860 Mary lived with forty-eight-year-old Richard Mills, who was also a stock raiser, as were five of their children: three males, aged twenty-four, twenty, and eighteen, and two females, Nancy A., sixteen, and Sarah H., fourteen. Mary Mills did not declare property taxes, which was not unusual for a married woman at that time, but it was possibly included in her husband's entry of "Mills, R. and Son." Mary and her daughters were identified as stock raisers in the census, but tax records show that the women owned nothing while the men claimed the property. Was this a case of mistaken job descriptions on the census records? Perhaps when the census taker inquired about Richard's profession, he responded with something like "I raise stock; we all do," or perhaps Mary stated that she and the older children helped Richard raise the stock. Perhaps she had sold her stock to help support the family? We can only speculate, but, like Margaret Brown and Rachel Brown, Mary Mills and her daughters participated in the livestock industry, but the focus was on the men in her household, not the women.[6]

When comparing Rachel Brown's and Mary Mills's records, the instinctive thought is that their husbands were the ones involved with livestock. One might also think that Mary Mills's involvement was minimal because there was only the one notation of her participation in the industry, in the census. While this may seem like a point unworthy of further consideration, it is unknown whether Mary or Richard initiated involvement in the livestock trade; it is just presumed that it was Richard. One could also ask the question that if the reverse was true—if Richard was listed as a stock raiser in the census, but his wife reported the stock on the tax records—would he still be perceived as the stock raiser? The short answer is yes, he would.

In *Texas Women on the Cattle Trails*, historian Sara R. Massey wrote, "Historians of the cattle drives have focused on the men—the dangers they faced, the challenges they overcame, and their ultimate success in profiting from the sale of cattle in the markets."[7] While it is indisputably true that men were the overwhelming participants in the livestock industry, both on the range and on the trail, conditioning and the continual allocation of gendered tasks during the antebellum years persuades historians that women's roles in the industry were minimal, if any, especially when there was a man present. Mind-set and preconceived notions are additional contributing factors in the missing history of women's contributions to the early Texas livestock industry.

Another problem for researchers is that women frequently changed their last names. Mary Barksdale is but one example, again in Atascosa County. Property taxes for 1860 show Mary Barksdale with eighteen horses worth $540, two thousand head of cattle worth $12,000, and fifty-five sheep worth $165. Her total value that year was $12,705 ($386,000 when adjusted for 2018 inflation). Property taxes were recorded at the beginning of the year, and census records were taken around midyear. Mary Barksdale was not listed in the 1860 census returns for Atascosa County, but there was a Mary Donahoe. She listed no profession, was forty-five, claimed $3,400 in real estate, $18,170 in personal estate, and was from Tennessee. She is without doubt Mary Barksdale, although further research is needed to determine whether she was the mother or stepmother of the seven younger Barksdales living in her house, all whom were born in Texas and had attended school within the year. In 1870, Mary was once again listed as Mary Barksdale, identified as a fifty-seven-year-old woman from Tennessee, and her involvement with the livestock industry is again hidden, as her profession is recorded as "keeping house." Her property tax records, however, reflect her continued involvement in the livestock industry despite her gendered occupational assignment in the census. It is impossible to know how much women's history has been missed due to name changes, credit given to men instead of women, clerical choices, or other circumstances, but it has certainly happened.[8]

Some women, like Martha Loring, were seemingly thrust into the livestock industry when their spouses died. In late 1856 or early 1857, Martha and John Loring moved from Fannin County to Cooke County, in North Texas. John's 1856 property taxes in Fannin County suggest that they were living quite well before they relocated, but they only included thirty head of cattle.[9] By February 12, 1857, approximately six months after the move, John died.[10] Subsequently, far removed from her Fannin County home of at least a decade, Martha worked to support her large family of nine children and nine slaves. That year, along with other property, she declared seven hundred head of cattle worth $1, 800 as the administrator of John's estate. The tremendous increase in the number of cattle from the thirty John declared to the seven hundred Martha reported suggests that livestock opportunities in Cooke County were the impetus for the move and that John had made a serious investment in cattle before he died, leaving Martha in an enviable position. However, estate records show how it was Martha, not John, who was vested in cattle.[11]

John's death made Martha the second-largest rancher and fifth-largest slave owner in Cooke County, and she was finally listed in the property tax records as a person with stock. Four years later, Martha held the fifth-largest cattle holdings in Cooke County out of fifty taxpayers who reported one hundred head of cattle or more. Her eight hundred head of cattle worth $5,800 show the value of livestock during a time that was not traditionally associated with cattle economy. That same year she also paid taxes on 1,450 acres worth $4,260, eleven slaves worth $6,000 and eight horses worth $560.[12]

In 1862, remarried, she paid taxes as Mrs. Martha A. Moore, but from 1863 until 1868 her new husband Isaac reported their property, including the stock.[13] Isaac died in late 1868, and, a widow again, Martha reported to pay her taxes. That year, due to a clerical error, she was listed as "Martha A. Martha," with 1,310 acres worth $2,380, five horses worth $200, and one thousand head of cattle worth $4,000. Much of the land was the same as she and John had owned in 1857, indicating that she had retained a portion of her real estate throughout the years she was married to Isaac, but it appears that the missing acreage was the most improved and valuable and had probably been sold to supplement income.[14]

Martha's story undoubtedly mirrors those of many other women involved in the livestock industry. Records of her activity only came to light with the passing of her husbands. The only identifier that suggests her involvement in the trade was in the 1880 census, three years before she died, when "keeping stock" was listed as her profession. In Cooke County, her surname was listed as Loring, Moore, and even Martha, which adds to the burden of tracing her history. Two years after Isaac died, she reverted to "Martha Loring" in the 1870 census, but in the 1880 return she was listed as M. A. Moore. Despite this, her headstone shows no relationship to Isaac Moore but harks back to her first husband in stating: "Martha, Wife of John Loring, Born Octo. 17, 1816, Died Dec. 5, 1883."[15] Martha is representative of the difficulties and challenges in researching women's history. Men generally have one surname throughout their lives, making them much easier to find in the records. Clerical errors, complete omission or misrepresentation in the records, name changes, and lost records are all common hurdles to cross when reconstructing women's contributions.

Other women in the livestock industry are scattered through the 1860 census returns. In Bell County, the sixteen-year-old daughter of L. Dikes [Dyches], was listed as a stock herder. Undoubtedly kin to William Dyches who left land and livestock to his heirs, the young woman is listed only as F. Dikes and represents another lost story. In Burnet County, Hannah Collins, a twenty-year-old woman from Mississippi with a six-month-old son, was listed as head of household. Hannah was not listed in the Burnet County property tax records for 1860, but her personal estate was listed at $7,000 on the census. Nothing more could readily be found about her at this time. Farther north in Comanche County two women were listed as stock raisers. The first, Louisa Sneed, was a thirty-nine-year-old from Tennessee with $3,200 in personal property. The list of people for whom she was the head of household and undoubtedly the provider suggests that she had been widowed or divorced from a man named Gorman and had seven children from that union. For all of these women, with or without children or a spouse, livestock afforded them opportunity in the antebellum economy, but their participation is overlooked in historical accounts.[16]

The second woman listed in Comanche County was Harriet Pippin. Harriet was twenty-three, had been to school, and was from Alabama, and she was also listed as one of the residents of John Baggett's house. Harriet's first marriage had been to Wiley Baggett, John's brother, on March 5, 1853, in DeSoto Parish, Louisiana. Harriet became widowed when Wiley died on December 6, 1857, leaving her to care for their two children, Wiley Jr. and Sarah. Wiley Sr. did not declare any livestock the year he died, but he did own four slaves worth $2,000. The following year the widowed Harriet appears in the tax records with no slaves, two horses worth $150, and 240 head of cattle worth $1,440; in 1859 she had 250 head of cattle worth $1,500. Without conducting research in the Comanche County courthouse, it cannot be conclusively stated that she sold the slaves to invest in cattle, but her tax records suggest that is what happened.[17]

About 1858, Harriet married William Carrol Pippin in what appears to have been a bad match, as she was residing with her former brother-in-law, John Baggett, just two years later when she also listed her profession as a stock raiser. Harriet is not listed in the 1860, 1861, or 1862 property taxes, but "W. C. Pippin" is, with no cattle. William enlisted with the Twenty-Fourth Cavalry in 1862. Suggesting that she had kept her own cattle but did not declare it during those missing tax years, much like Martha Loring, Harriet reemerged with 350 head worth $2,100 in 1863, and in 1864 she had $1,200 in livestock property. Also of interest is that she is listed as having attended school within the year on the census report, a common thread among many ranching women and their children and another point to consider when discussing the generalities associated with livestock traders, as they are often relegated to the lower classes of southern society. What school she attended and why she was attending as a newly married woman raise more questions. Perhaps she used her education to get out of the livestock trade, explaining why she cannot be found in the tax records after 1864. Or perhaps she remarried, moved, or died—a distinct possibility since William married again sometime in 1868. Much like Lucinda Walker's story, Harriett Pippin's is laden with unanswerable questions.[18]

A hindrance to identification of men and women involved in the livestock trade during the period in question is the use of the all-encompassing term "farmer" used to denote profession in the 1850 and 1860 censuses. The term suggests a person who tilled the land, raised some kind of crop or livestock, and lived in a rural area, but it is problematic for those trying to identify the actual number of people who depended on livestock for the majority of their income. Additionally, one could argue that the term has contributed to the underrepresentation of the economic role of livestock before 1866 and perhaps after, because it undercounts the people who primarily depended on livestock for their main income.

In Victoria County, Margaret Heffernan Dunbar Hardy married her third husband, Alexander Borland, on February 11, 1856. Although multiple sources state that Borland was a rich rancher, there is no evidence that supports this assertion. If anything, the evidence shows that Margaret was the rich rancher who married a poor man. Borland is not listed in Victoria County's property tax records until 1856, when he declared no taxable property whatsoever. That same year Margaret declared four horses worth $200 and fifteen hundred head of cattle valued at $7,500—the same as her holdings in 1855, and one more horse than in 1854. The year after they were married, his property taxes were listed under "Borland, Alex and wife" and more accurately reflect her earlier declarations, not his: three horses worth $75 and two thousand head of cattle worth $12,000. Further evidence of her wealth being transferred to Borland appears in the 1860 census, where his entry shows the all-encompassing term "farming" as his profession and credits him with $14,500 in real estate and $28,000 in personal property; Margaret is listed without a profession or property. His tax records from that year show that the cattle now numbered thirty-five hundred and were worth $21,000; additionally, there were at least three slaves, Louisa, John, and Emily, who actually belonged to Margaret.[19]

Harrison Dunbar, Margaret's first husband, had owned thirty head of cattle and possibly a house in Victoria before he died "shortly after the birth of their daughter, Mary, . . . in a pistol duel on the streets of Victoria." Her second husband, Milton H. Hardy, owned substantial real and personal property including slaves and livestock before he

Figure 4. Margaret Heffernan Dunbar Hardy Bourland with her
straw hat on her lap, circa 1872. General Photograph Collection,
from Lender Celeste Hopkins Brown, UTSA Special Collections.

died from cholera in August 1852. The list of items in Hardy's estate
appraisal is impressive, including nearly fifteen hundred head of cattle, and, though most of his estate did not initially go to Margaret, it
soon did, along with a settlement from her father's estate. Historian
Phyllis McKenzie wrote, "Some of [the livestock that were attributed
to Alexander Borland in 1860] may have been Margaret's inheritance
from either her father [Heffernan] or Hardy, for in later years she
consistently used the "H" brand in her ranching operations." Thus,
it is accurate to say that most if not all of Borland's livestock were
Margaret's, not his.[20]

When the Civil War began, Borland enlisted as a private in the Victoria Cavalry Company for coastal defense with other "married men and men unable to go into active service." He lived through the war but passed away in the spring of 1867, leaving Margaret a widow for the third time. The year before he died he declared three thousand head of cattle worth $15,000; the year after he died, Margaret declared four thousand head worth $12,000. In 1873, Margaret Borland became one of the first women to drive cattle up the Chisholm Trail to sell her stock in Kansas, a decision that may have cost her life, as she died shortly after the drive. Throughout her adult life the one constant was livestock—her father's, her husbands', and her own. Margaret is yet another example of a woman who was widowed multiple times, but rather than become a victim of her circumstances she capitalized on inherited livestock to become a wealthy rancher. She is also another example of a woman whose holdings were credited to a man. Mr. Borland was not a wealthy rancher who married a poor widow—it was just the opposite.[21]

Opportunities in the livestock industry were not restricted by ethnicity. Listed as head of households in consecutive 1860 Jackson County homes were two "mulatta" sisters and their families. Harriet Reynolds lived in dwelling number 230 with eight other residents; next door was Margaret "Hulda" McCulloch, with twelve other residents in her home, including her mother Rose and sister Jane. All four of these women were the former property of Samuel McCulloch, and the three sisters were his biological offspring. Emancipated in 1835, they moved from Alabama to Texas with McCulloch. All four women were listed as stock raisers in the 1860 census, with a combined $5,000 in real estate and $8,870 in personal property. The property taxes show that without Hulda's total included (she did not report that year) they claimed thirty-eight horses worth $1,400 and 850 head of cattle worth $5,000: Jane owned fourteen horses worth $500 and 250 head of cattle worth $1,500, Ann owned ten horses worth $400 and 350 head of cattle worth $2,000, and Harriett owned fourteen horses worth $500 and 250 head of cattle worth $1,500.[22] For these free black women living in a southern state, livestock provided an equal economic opportunity where chances for employment and upward mobility were limited by the color of their skin.

One of the better-known Texas women from this time is Elizabeth FitzPatrick. Elizabeth is known more for being a victim than for being a survivor, but she and her family would not have been the target of the Elm Creek Raid had she not been a success in the cattle industry. On October 13, 1864, a group of Kiowa and Comanche Indians attacked her ranch home in Young County, killing and kidnapping black and white women and their children.[23] The details that are omitted from most of the historical accounts of this raid show why the home was a target in the first place. Unlike Lucinda Walker, there is evidence that Elizabeth worked in the ranching industry long before the era of the postwar cattle drives to northern markets.

Elizabeth's tax records show the activity and increase in her property throughout the years as she accumulated, maintained, and participated in early Texas ranching (see table). Elizabeth was one of four brides in Young County during 1862; it was her third marriage. Her first marriage had ended when her husband, Alexander Carter, and father-in-law, Edmund J. Carter, both free mulattos, were murdered in September 1857. Before he died, her father-in-law reputedly owned a ranch where Elizabeth had not worked, and she became a controlling partner and manager of both ranch hands and cattle after Alexander's death.[24]

Despite Elizabeth's obvious ability, her husband's estate was managed by a man and controlled by the all-white male judicial system, limiting what she could and could not do. Aside from legal issues pertaining to the ranch, she was unable to obtain legal guardianship over her own son, Elijah, due to her tendency to have epileptic seizures. She fought for five years with and against two different male administrators—who both died—and finally won her case and obtained guardianship of Elijah not long before she was made to watch him burn alive during the Indian's retreat after the Elm Creek Raid.[25]

Elizabeth's property tax records show a woman who was very much involved in the livestock economy on the Texas frontier. From the year her first husband died through her second and third marriages, she consistently declared large holdings; additionally, her second and third husbands did not report ownership of any cattle before they married her. Elizabeth, like many other women in Texas, was a successful rancher before and throughout the war years. She not only managed

Table. Property taxes of Elizabeth Carter Sprague FitzPatrick

Name	Year	Horses	Cattle
Carter, E. A.	1857	9 ($675)	700 ($4,900)
Sprague, Elizabeth	1858	9 ($540)	822 ($6,150)
Sprague, Elizabeth	1859	3 ($150)	754 ($4,580)
Sprague, Elizabeth	1860	3 ($200)	804 [$3,000]
Sprigg, Elizabeth	1861	2 ($70)	800 ($4,800)
FitzPatrick, Thomas	1862	1 ($90)	0
Spriggs, E.	1862	5 ($250)	900 ($4,500)
FitzPatrick, Thomas	1863	Property value	$370
FitzPatrick, Elizabeth	1863	Total property value	$10,050
FitzPatrick, E. J.	1864	Total livestock	$7,000

Source: Young County property taxes, 1857–1864, University of North Texas

men in the ranching industry but also capitalized on economic opportunities offered by the livestock industry.

Several common threads through this brief study should be noted. Age and ethnicity did not prevent these few women from participating in the livestock economy. Single, married, widowed, and remarried women all engaged in the industry. Marriage and name changes make it difficult to compile data. Many women ranchers were educated, and some had children who had attended school. Livestock offered the possibility of accumulating significant wealth during a time when career paths for women were limited. Therefore, the industry offered the same opportunities to women as to men of the same ilk, but tracing women's participation presents a unique set of challenges.

What began as a search to learn about Lucinda Walker has uncovered other women who were engaged in the Texas livestock trade before the end of the Civil War. Historians have paid little attention to the Texas cattle industry before the era of the Chisholm Trail and the postwar drives, much less how women contributed or benefited from the industry. Except for Lucinda, the women in this chapter were found in less than a few hours of reading through a handful of counties' census records, pointing to the large numbers that could be uncovered by a dedicated researcher. These women were daughters, wives, mothers, and widows who, just like the men around them, took advantage of an industry that was not gender-aware and that offered alternate opportunities to those who would take it. How many others are missing from the histories of early Texas will surely never be known, but it can be surmised that many women were an integral component of the economic machine in those early years of settlement and that more work needs to be done to represent them in the historical record.

Notes

The author is profoundly grateful to Carla Tate Deaton Williams for introducing her to the world of women in ranching. She would also like to thank Helen Dill for editorial comments.

1. Abstract of Purchases at Red River Station for November 1862, File 838–17, Quartermaster Returns, Red River Station, 1862, Box 401–838, Texas State Archives, Austin. The author would like to thank David Murrah for suggestions and help with this chapter.

2. Eighth Census of the United States, Polk County, Texas, Schedule 1 (Free Population), University of North Texas; "Red River Station, " *Historical Bytes*, https: //historicalbytes.wordpress.com/tag/montague-county/page/2. Many thanks to Keith Volanto for help locating Lucinda Walkers in multiple locations.

3. The 1862 total of $47.15 is the equivalent of $1,190 in 2017. See MeasuringWorth.com

4. A complete search of all antebellum counties in the state of Texas was not conducted for this article, which leaves an open door for a much more detailed study.

5. Eighth Census of the United States, Atascosa County, Texas, Schedule 1 (Free Population), University of North Texas (hereafter UNT); Atascosa County property tax records, 1859–1860, UNT.

6. Other women in the 1860 Atascosa County census are identified as stock raisers. Jane Umphries [Humphries?] from Louisiana, was a sixty-one-year-old head of household. Elizabeth, nineteen; John, eighteen and also listed as stock raiser; and James, fourteen, were all living with her. No tax records could be found for Jane. Marier [Maria?] L. Delgado, from Texas, a thirty-three-year-old stock raiser, was head of household over Jose, seventeen, stock raiser, and five other boys ranging from nine months to seventeen years old. Delgado cannot be found listed in the property tax records. Mary J. Barnes, a thirty-two-year-old head of household from Mississippi, is also listed as stock raiser, with one boy, eleven, and two girls, nine and seven. No tax records were found for Mary Barnes. Mary L. Bright, from Alabama, was a twenty-eight-year-old head of household. There were two children in her home: Charles, eight, and William T., four. There was also James McCrea, forty-seven, who was listed as a doctor. Mary Bright's taxes reflect success. She had 320 acres worth $1,300, four lots in

Pleasanton worth $150, two slaves worth $2,000, one hundred horses valued at $4,000, and four hundred head of cattle worth $2,400. Her combined value was a substantial $10,155. The last woman listed is Elizabeth Miller, head of household, fifty-eight, from Louisiana. She had four other stock-raising family members living with her, three men from aged twenty-one to thirty, and a woman, Mary, twenty-years. She does not appear in the tax records. Eighth Census of the United States, Atascosa County, Texas, Schedule 1 (Free Population), UNT; Atascosa County property tax records, 1859–1860, UNT.

7. Sara R. Massey, *Texas Women on the Cattle Trails* (College Station: Texas A&M Press, 2006), 4.

8. Eighth Census of the United States, Atascosa County, Texas, Schedule 1 (Free Population), UNT; Atascosa County property tax records, 1859–1860, UNT; Ninth Census of the United States, Atascosa County, Texas, UNT.

9. Fannin County property taxes, 1856, UNT.

10. The consensus seems to be that a drunken John was whipping his one-armed slave, Jack, for cutting firewood too slowly. During the whipping, Jack's axe became entangled in the whip and fatally struck John in the head. Family lore says that Martha spoke up for Jack in court, although no records have yet been found to verify this. Support for Martha's testimony can be found in Cooke County's 1866 tax records, where a "Loring, Jack (Freedman)" is listed, as well as in an account of "a one armed negro called Old Jack Loring," in Fannie Potter, *History of Montague County* (Austin, Tex: E. L. Steck, 1912), 25.

11. Cooke County property taxes, 1857, UNT.

12. Cooke County property taxes, 1857, UNT; Index and Marriage Records, 2, 1858–1872, UNT; Ninth Census of the United States, UNT; Estate Records for I. A. Moore, box 22, Cooke County Clerk's office, Denton, Texas. Those who declared more than her were W. H. Donner with 1,380 cattle, Samuel Doss with 5,000, the partnership of James and W. Peery with 2,200, and J. D. Black, who had an agent report his 1,822 head. Doss and Peery were influential in the Great Hanging of 1862 in Gainesville, Cooke County (forty-one suspected Unionists were hanged there in October that year), which speaks to the influence livestock raisers held within their community. For more about the Great Hanging, see Richard B. McCaslin, *Tainted Breeze: The Great Hanging at Gainesville, Texas 1862* (Baton Rouge: Louisiana State University Press, 1994).

13. Probate records of John Loring, box 10, Cooke County, County Clerk's office, Denton, Texas.

14. John Nathaniel "Jack" Loring, FindAGrave.com, accessed January 25, 2016, http://www.findagrave.com/memorial/150956381/john-nathaniel-loring. For more about Martha, see Deborah Liles, "Martha Alice Loring: An Unlikely Woman on the Texas Frontier," *Central Texas Studies: The Journal of the Central Texas Historical Association* 2 (December 2017): 9–24.

15. Cooke County property tax records, 1857–1868, UNT; Ninth and Tenth Census of the United States, Cooke County, UNT; "Martha Alice Landers Loring," FindAGrave.com, accessed January 25, 2016, https://www.findagrave.com/memorial/150958242/martha-alice-loring.

16. Eighth Census of the United States, Bell County, Texas, Schedule 1 (Free Population), UNT; Property tax rolls, Bell County, 1859–1861, UNT; Eighth Census of the United States, Burnett County, Texas, Schedule 1 (Free Population), UNT; Eighth Census of the United States, Comanche County, Texas, Schedule 1 (Free Population), UNT.

17. "Marriage Records, 1837–1860, Surnames A–K, DeSoto Parish, Louisiana," Rootsweb, accessed February 6, 2016, http://files.usgwarchives.net/la/desoto/vitals/marriages/1837ak.txt; Property tax rolls, Comanche County, 1857–1859, UNT. Many thanks to Ruth Karbach for assistance with Pippin's records.

18. "Harriet Spears m Wiley Baggett," Family Search, accessed February 6, 2016, https: //familysearch.org/learn/wiki/en/Comanche_County, _ Texas_ Genealogy; Eighth Census of the United States, Comanche County, Texas, Schedule 1 (Free Population); William C. Pippin, Texas, Civil War Service Records of Confederate Soldiers FamilySearch.org, accessed February 6, 2016, https: //familysearch.org/ark: /61903/1: 1: FZ4Y-N5G; Property tax rolls, Comanche County, 1857–1864.

19. Victoria County property tax records, 1854–1868, quotation from 1857, UNT; Eighth census of the United States, Victoria County, Schedule 1 (Free Population).

20. Phyllis A. McKenzie, "Margaret Heffernan Dunbar Hardy Borland: Mrs. Alexander Borland," in *Texas Women on the Cattle Trails*, Sara R. Massey, ed. (College Station: Texas A&M University Press, 2006), 97–106, first quotation from 97, second quotation from 100; "Estate of Milton H. Hardy," Probate Minutes, Vol. 2a, 1849–1867, Victoria, Texas, Ancestry.com, accessed February 16, 2016.

21. Quotation from "Alex Borland, Civil War Index—Abstracts of Muster Rolls," Ancestry.com, accessed March 6, 2016; Victoria County property tax records, 1854–1868, UNT; McKenzie, "Margaret Heffernan Dunbar Hardy Borland," 103–6.

22. Eighth Census of the United States, Jackson County, Texas, Schedule 1 (Free population), UNT; "Brief Biography of Margaret Hulda McCulloch," FamilySearch.org, accessed December 7, 2015; Jackson County property tax records, 1860, UNT. For a little perspective, these three free women owned more than $152,000 in livestock in 2017 equivalency See MeasuringWorth.com.

23. Patricia Adkins-Rochette, *Borland in North Texas and Indian Territory during the Civil War: Fort Cobb, Fort Arbuckle & the Wichita Mountains* (Broken Arrow, Okla., 2005), 277–81. Testimonies from the grown children and another captive woman are recorded in this version of the event.

24. Young County property tax records, 1857. According to Barbara Ledbetter, Edmund J. Carter, Elizabeth's father-in-law, was the wealthiest man in Young County, with "ten times more property than even the county judge of the county . . . land, oxen, mules, wagons, dwelling, money, 700 head of cattle, and nine horses." There are no property tax records to support this claim, as Carter did not report in 1857. See Barbara A. Neal Ledbetter, *Fort Belknap Frontier Saga: Indians, Negroes and Anglo-Americans on the Texas Border* (Burnet,

Tex: Eakin Press, 1982), 33, 61, 87, 103–6. Alex Carter, his father "Edward" [Edmund] J., and Eliza's daughter Milliard are listed as mulattos in the Navarro County census for 1850. Neither man declared property taxes, which makes it difficult to verify their wealth. Not only did Elizabeth survive the murder of her husband and father-in-law but she would have also had to deal with the stigma of being in a biracial marriage during the antebellum years.

25. Ledbetter, *Fort Belknap Frontier Saga*, 103–6.

Chapter 3

Cornelia Adair

Transatlantic Panhandle Rancher

Alex Hunt

Cornelia Wadsworth Ritchie Adair was a remarkable woman who owned and managed the Paloduro Ranch, better known as the JA Ranch, in the Texas Panhandle. The JA Ranch holds a place of importance in Texas history since it is associated with legendary figures like Charles Goodnight and Quanah Parker. Further, as a model of British investment in Great Plains ranching, the JA holds a significant place in the history of economic development of the American West. Adair was a native of New York State, lived primarily in London and Ireland, and became a British subject. While she visited her JA Ranch many times between her coming into its ownership in 1885 and her death in 1921 and kept a residence in Clarendon, Texas, she was an absentee owner and long-distance manager. However, Adair was no dilettante but was heavily involved in all aspects of JA operations, including management of personnel, livestock, land, and finances. Moreover, she had a great and genuine love for the JA.

Naturally, much about Cornelia Adair's life falls outside the scope of this project's focus on ranching. But, in brief, it is important to know that her life was one of many interests, high society, and travel. She frequently visited New York City and western New York State, where her family, powerfully connected in US politics, was based. She spent much of her time in her fashionable house in London; a cottage in Rathdaire,

Ireland, that was her late husband's family seat; and her Glenveagh Castle in Donegal, Ireland, where she entertained royalty and men high in politics. She later built a retirement home too, in Bath, England. Along with Jennie Churchill and other American women in England, she became involved in a successful effort to send a US hospital ship to assist the British in the Boer War in South Africa in 1899. She was a great traveler; capping her life of adventure, she traveled to India at the age of sixty-six as the guest of her friend and frequent visitor Lord Herbert Kitchener, commander-in-chief of the British army in India, on the occasion of the Delhi Durbar in 1903. Thus, her Texas ranch was but one part, albeit an important part, of Adair's life.

Figure 5. Cornelia Adair. Courtesy of Panhandle-Plains Historical Museum Research Center.

Cornelia Adair's cosmopolitanism and her gender have led to historians' struggle to characterize her role in management of the JA. The Canyon, Texas, newspaper announced her arrival at the ranch in 1901 by referring to her as "the English cattle queen."[1] A subsequent report detailed Cornelia's riding with the outfit during the branding at the ranch's Tule division: "She will be with the cowboys during this week. She is an expert rider and has her horses and saddle and will do a great deal of riding at the roundup."[2] Cornelia did not rope cattle or mend fence, but she loved to ride and was keen to observe ranch operations. Ultimately she was a rancher, not just a ranch owner, for if the combination of knowledge of ranches and cattle and a love of place make one a rancher, she deserves the title.

Adair was born Cornelia Wadsworth in 1837 to a wealthy and powerful family based in the Genesee Valley of upstate New York. The family owned a great deal of land and, while having many business connections and a vested interest in politics, kept a strong foundation in the business of ranching and farming. Growing up, Cornelia learned about work on a farm and not only how to ride but also how to care for and judge livestock. Long after her death, her friend M. K. Brown would remark perceptively, "In thinking back about Mrs. Adair and the whole Wadsworth family, it is interesting to me to note that their interests touched every facet of life, yet they remained essentially a people of the land—farmers, dairymen, cattle raisers, and such. They delved into a multitude of business ventures and politics, always politics. Yet they never released their contact and kinship with the land."[3] This background would prove important to Cornelia's decision to retain the JA despite numerous opportunities to sell it.

As a young woman, Cornelia became a beauty well known in society. Her first husband, Montgomery Ritchie, died in 1864 after serving in the Civil War. In 1867 she married John George Adair, a Scotch-Irish landowner and financier. Like Cornelia, Adair had a family background in agriculture, and he had become a major landowner in Ireland, infamous for evictions of tenant farmers. The couple divided their time between Ireland and New York. In the fall of 1874, John and Cornelia took a tour of the western prairies of Nebraska. The trip, which featured a buffalo hunt and a visit to a Sioux encampment, impressed upon the Adairs the grandeur and expanse of the West and was important in implanting the idea of getting into the western cattle business.

Cornelia kept a diary of the trip. Published in 1918, it reveals her view of the world, conditioned by wealth and privilege, particularly her perspective of class and bias against those she considered her inferiors —the Irish, Chinese, blacks, and poor people in general. She wrote, "Wherever one travels in America, this extraordinary restlessness of the people strikes one. Whole families move hither and thither in every direction, trying first one thing and then another until they meet fortune in some shape. One could not help pitying these poor people in the train to-day, though they made one very uncomfortable."[4] But despite her discomforts, she opened herself to experience and adventure.

A highpoint of Cornelia's trip was her party's visit, accompanied by a military escort, to the Oglala Lakota camp (Cornelia referred to them as "Sioux Indians").[5] Cornelia's account demonstrates fear and revulsion but also positive sentiments. She found "Chief Two Lance" a "natural gentleman" but noted that "cunning and cruelty were said to be his special characteristics." "Mrs. Two Lance," Cornelia wrote, "rode up to our tent sitting on a man's saddle, but quite at ease, as a Queen should be," and Cornelia noted beautiful beadwork but also "the filthiest old short calico petticoat" the woman wore. Cornelia reflected, "It is all like a dream, it seems too strange to be true, that I should see these uncivilized Indians now really for the first time in my life, when I return to America almost as a foreigner."[6] She also noted significantly, "We passed several large ranches: the small low houses attached to a large corral, and surrounded by enormous hayricks. All along the South Platte, within the last few years, these enormous cattle-ranches have been established. One man has a herd of 30,000; they are very profitable."[7] In Cornelia's musings, perhaps, are the seeds of the JA.

Because of advantageous exchange rates in the United States, John George Adair had relocated his brokerage business to New York. By all accounts a man difficult to get along with, John seems to have had friction with his Wadsworth in-laws and soon traveled farther west, moving his business to Denver.[8] Seeking opportunity, he was introduced to Charles Goodnight, at that time greatly in need of capital, and the two went into partnership to form the JA Ranch. On the Adairs' first visit to their new property in 1877, Cornelia rode horseback—sidesaddle—from Pueblo, Colorado, to the JA, a distance of four hundred miles. They spent two weeks' time visiting before returning, again with a US cavalry escort.[9]

John Adair died unexpectedly in 1885, and Cornelia became Goodnight's partner. Most commentators assert that Cornelia would become more engaged in JA affairs than John had ever been. Cornelia's partnership with Goodnight would end in 1887 (see below), and she would continue as sole owner of the ranch for the next thirty-three years. Historian Frances Vick notes that at this point "Cornelia became one of the few women in the world to preside over such a huge enterprise and financial empire."[10]

The JA reached its apex under Cornelia's ownership. By 1887 the ranch had grown to over six hundred thousand acres owned and, all told, over 1.3 million acres grazed.[11] The original JA range—known as the Paloduro Ranch (a name that Cornelia used in preference to "JA" to refer to the entirety of her Texas property)—with the addition of the Tule Ranch and the Quitaque Ranch covered portions of Armstrong, Randall, Donley, Briscoe, Swisher, Floyd, and Hall Counties. In 1888, the JA had the most cattle that it ever would, with 60,759 mature animals and a calf crop of 12,654.[12] While the size of the range and number of cattle subsequently declined, from the 1890s through the 1910s the JA became a more consolidated property, with a higher-quality product, its fenced pastures producing nationally recognized beef cattle. In its early period under Goodnight's management, 1878–88, the JA drove cattle up the trail to railheads. The main product was steers, typically at two or three years of age, as well as culled cows. After the last drive, in 1888, the same general practices persisted, but marketing was handled locally. In the 1910s, the JA became what it continues to be in the twenty-first century, primarily a cow-calf beef operation, in which an established herd produces calves that are marketed at about six months old, as the primary income of the ranch.[13] Goodnight began the JA herd by introducing blooded Durham or Shorthorn bulls to Texas longhorn cattle, but beginning in 1882 and persisting long after Cornelia Adair's time, the breeding bulls of the high-grade JJ or American Herd were Herefords, the most popular cattle breed of the period.[14] The JA continues under the ownership of Cornelia Adair's great-granddaughter Cornelia Wadsworth Ritchie and is the longest-running privately owned ranch in the Texas Panhandle.[15]

Not surprisingly, Cornelia Adair engaged assistants in financial and legal matters on both sides of the Atlantic. Arthur Renshaw, member of a wealthy and politically influential family in England, visited the JA with the Adairs in the early 1880s and subsequently, with encouragement from Mrs. Adair, founded the Texas Land and Mortgage Company of Dundee, Scotland, which would partly fund JA land financing, even as John George Adair served as a director.[16] Two years after John Adair's death in1885, Cornelia hired the Texas Land and Mortgage Company (TLMC) as financial agent and managers of the JA and Tule Ranches on her behalf. An agent of the TLMC came to the ranch from Dallas every six weeks.[17]

Cornelia also hired a number of on-the-ground managers to run the JA. Following Goodnight, the managers were J. E. Farrington (1887–90), Arthur Tisdale (1890–91), Richard "Dick" Walsh (1892–1910), John Summerfield (1910–11), James W. Wadsworth Jr. (1911–1915), and finally T. D. Hobart, hired in 1915. Hobart served as manager while acting as co-executor of Cornelia's will after her death in 1921; that messy job would continue after *his* death in 1935.[18] Cornelia's son James Wadsworth "Jack" Ritchie worked at the JA and was briefly the Tule division manager of the before being dismissed by Goodnight for gambling and drinking with his men at the ranch.[19]

Despite establishing these layers of management, Cornelia Adair remained in control of ranch affairs and visited often. Based on assessment of various records—correspondence, newspaper accounts, travel manifests, and so on—clearly Cornelia visited the ranch most years, typically arriving in October or November and staying until January or February.[20] Though the record is patchy, existing documents demonstrate Cornelia's unflagging engagement with ranch affairs via correspondence with her financial agents and ranch employees.

Scholars of the JA typically focus on Charles Goodnight and tend to give short shrift to Cornelia Adair's role as ranch manager or as agent of her own affairs. An excellent example of her business sense and of historians' evolving recognition of it centers on the circumstances and negotiations of her split with Goodnight in 1887. By 1886 Goodnight already seemed to be, as he later put it to Cornelia, "heartily sick of men and ranches."[21] That year Goodnight argued that the coming of railroads and farmers would make the ranch unprofitable—and that they should sell. Short of that, Goodnight wanted out. He proposed to take one-third of the ranch, but in the end he settled for the Quitaque division, consisting of 140,000 acres, and twenty thousand cattle. Cornelia kept the JA's primary Palo duro Ranch and the more recent Tule addition. In his 1926 *History the JA Ranch*, Harley True Burton merely stated facts about the 1887 split: "Mrs. Adair traded him this [Quitaque] ranch for his third interest in the JA Ranch and traded him the cattle—about twenty thousand head—for his third interest in the cattle on the JA Ranch."[22] (Burton includes a statement from Goodnight that, in 1882, "Adair got me to buy the Quitaque Ranch for Mrs. Adair," raising the question of whether the wealthy widow Cornelia provided the funds.)[23]

Goodnight biographer J. Evetts Haley at more length explains that Goodnight made a bad deal. Mrs. Adair sent William Maquay, a banker in Florence, Italy, and according to Haley an illegitimate son of John George Adair, to negotiate on her behalf. Haley wrote that Cornelia's "indecision" on the question of selling the ranch "had driven [Goodnight] into taking the losing end to assure the trade's going through. But the partnership had not been pleasant, conditions were terribly adverse, and he was anxious to close out while he yet had time."[24] Haley also notes that these were "hard negotiations," and Goodnight had many other troubles on his mind. In any case, Haley claims, Goodnight was subsequently bitter at "his misfortune in division" and considered "his greatest mistake . . . leaving the rugged JA's."[25] In his bitterness, Goodnight's view of events may tend to show Cornelia in a poor light and minimize his own lack of business acumen. In any case, Haley's sympathies were with Goodnight, the subject of his biography, rather than with Cornelia.

Alternatively, in William Hagan's brief biography of Goodnight, a story is retold that rightfully gives Cornelia more credit. Hagan writes that Cornelia, far from indecisive, was a "canny businesswoman with great experience in landholding in the United States and the United Kingdom." He points out the obvious: "She was not pressing him to sell out, but if he insisted, it would be on her terms. . . . [T]he partnership contract gave her first choice if it were dissolved, and she apparently had the final say on how the boundaries of the divisions were drawn."[26] Goodnight was right about the influx of small farmers on the range, but Cornelia nevertheless proved that the ranch could survive the changing times.

Moving forward, Cornelia's correspondence with ranch employees indicates that she required regular reports from the ranch—not only from the ranch manager but also from others, including foremen and accountants, whomever she could compel to write. She made it clear that she was eager for news of the ranch and valued multiple perspectives. Also, whether by design or by happenstance, it seems that Cornelia ran a tight ship by corresponding with multiple employees rather than receiving information only from the manager in a strict chain-of-command model. She was also extremely tactful, often admonishing her manager to handle personnel matters in a way to minimize "friction."[27]

A telling letter from George F. Walker, JA bookkeeper, to Cornelia on October 6, 1892, came just at the end of Arthur Tisdale's very short time as manager and as Dick Walsh was moving up into the position. Clearly recovering from a scolding, Walker wrote, "In future I will furnish you copies of the account sales of cattle as they occur and any other business transactions on the ranch." He concluded in part, "I regret very much that I failed to please you with my letters. . . . Mr. Tisdale informs me that you wish me to continue writing to you fortnightly. Although there is nothing in my agreement about writing you once a fortnight, I am quite willing to continue doing so, if I can satisfy you with what information I can furnish, or anything else that lies in my power, I will willingly do to assist in the Ranch business."[28] Thereafter indeed Walker reported regularly, detailing cattle sales primarily but also including other financial information and notes about weather, bounties paid on wolves, and other matters.

When Walsh took over management of the ranch in December

1893, regular reports continued. Mrs. Adair seems to have had great confidence in Walsh, who came to Texas from Dublin to work at the JA in 1885 and remained her friend long after he left in 1910. Walsh is credited with the work of consolidating the ranch by negotiating settlements with small farmers or "nesters" who settled on the ranch's rangelands.[29] He is also known for his work in improving the quality of the JA herd to the degree that its steers won the 1901 grand championship at the International Live Stock Exposition in Chicago and a similar award at the St. Louis World's Fair in 1904.[30]

A surviving letter from Walsh to Adair from April 1896 suggests the ease between them. Among numerous other matters, Walsh detailed several ongoing land purchases and exchanges that would consolidate the JA's Mulberry Pasture. He wrote:

> I have just returned from a trip all over the Paloduro Range having visited all the camps and I never saw the cattle looking better at this time of year. There has been no loss last winter except what died from natural causes. The prospects of a large calf crop are very good. The wolves are not very bad just at present and in the last fortnight there have been 28 pups killed and one old wolf! . . . We are making arrangements to commence the Spring Roundup on the 20th of this month so we will have to deliver the two yr. olds by the 20th of May. I will send you an estimate next week of what money will be coming in and how much we will require and how much we can send you.[31]

Walsh's informal tone, like his long tenure with the JA itself, suggests his ease with his employer and her trust in him.

During Walsh's time, the JA cattle herd developed famously, but another difficult period of management transition ensued after he left the ranch in 1910. Cornelia's nephew James Wolcott Wadsworth Jr. visited her in 1910. On New Year's Eve of that year, she wrote to James, who had just lost an election as Republican candidate for lieutenant governor of New York; she knew he was temporarily "out of a job" and asked him to take over management of the ranch. She wrote: "Since you left I have been thinking so much about the way you grasped everything here, and seemed to understand the business well as if you had been at it all of your life. I wonder if it would suit you to take control of this property." Cornelia then went on to add a bit of flattery to sweeten the offer: "You took everybody by storm in this country. They cannot say enough about you. Of course, now for a year or so you may be out of politics, and this might amuse and interest you, and by the time you return to politics the whole property may be sold or you may have put it on such a basis that even if you were a Cabinet Minister it would walk by itself!" She closes with somewhat of a plea: "I know if you accept this proposal it would be the most supreme relief to my mind. Of course, I am not satisfied with Mr. Summerfield [manager briefly in 1910–11], "but I was in such a hole that I hardly knew where to turn."[32] Wadsworth did take some convincing. He was a man with a farm, a wife and small children, and much business in New York. He wrote to his mother that he had turned down the position.[33] But perhaps Cornelia appealed to her brother, whom James Jr. addresses as "Boss"; for whatever reason, Cornelia prevailed, and he took the job.[34]

When Wadsworth arrived at the JA to take over management in 1911, Cornelia was at the ranch. Wadsworth found her gravely ill and weak, having suffered the "grippe"—or flu. Seventy-four years old, she was well aware of her mortality. James reported to his wife "[She] is now so low as to cause great alarm. I confess I'm pessimistic about her ever leaving this place. . . . She is entirely content to die here and [said] she wants to be buried in the tiny cemetery near the house—in the centre of her beloved domain."[35] Cornelia recovered, however, and would live for ten more years.

Cornelia's control of ranch management, or her sense of being kept appraised of the business, was lessened during this period. Likely James Wadsworth Jr.'s status as a family member, one who had perhaps been somewhat pressed into service through family bonds, led to him feeling that he could be more aloof from Cornelia's demands. Wadsworth's tenure as ranch manager was also marked by difficulties caused by World War I. Among other things, travel became more difficult after the United States entered the war, and Cornelia was able to visit the JA less often, exacerbating her sense of exclusion. The end of Wadsworth's tenure at the JA came with a telegram in the summer of 1914 informing him that he had been nominated as New York's Republican candidate for US senator.[36] Cornelia managed a visit to the ranch over the winter of 1914 to engage a new manager and settled upon T. D. Hobart of the White Deer Land Company. After initially declining the position, he met with Cornelia and the two came to terms.[37]

Correspondence between Hobart and Adair from 1915 to 1920, invaluable in its breadth and scope, with hundreds of letters from each, provides an excellent demonstration of Cornelia's continuing interest and knowledge—at seventy-eight years of age and beyond—in JA affairs. In a long letter written upon Hobart's acceptance of the position, Cornelia demonstrated command of the operation. She declared herself satisfied with the current scheme with respect to cattle, stating that any alteration to livestock operations, as well as any planned sale of land, had to be approved by her. Significantly, she remarked that the JA was a "breeding Ranch." She continued, "I have no desire to simply take as much money out of the place as I can, but am keenly interested in its development and improvement, as I consider the prosperity of Texas is only now really beginning, and I suppose I have known the

Figure 6. Hunting party at the JA Ranch, circa 1890. *Left to right*: "Mr. Stevenson," Cornelia Adair, one of Cornelia's nieces, and ranch manager Richard Walsh. Courtesy of Panhandle-Plains Historical Museum Research Center.

conditions of the State longer than most people."[38] Cornelia showed some chutzpah here, but having arrived on the scene when it was still a wild frontier in 1877, her claim was justified.

She then went on to introduce Hobart to the staff—foreman, accountant, auditor—and included some assessment of personalities, strengths, weaknesses, and foibles that she obviously thought should inform Hobart's dealings. She noted that J. W. Kent, range foreman, was "very well thought of"; however, in a revealing bit of background, she explained that it had not always been so:

> In the interval between Mr. Walsh's departure and my appointing my nephew General Manager, Mr. Summerfield was General Manager. I did not like his influence on Kent and I parted with him (Kent) in 1911. He then lived on his own land for 2 ½ years and quite retrieved his character by steadiness and hard work. Everyone tells me that ever since 1911 he has never been known to be anything but steady. I had a very unsatisfactory Range Foreman [Reynolds] in his place and in January, 1914, I reinstated Kent, and have so far not regretted doing so. The improvement of cattle is really extraordinary. He is a very good judge of breeding and quality, and Mr. Wadsworth told me he had a very high opinion of him. As I think I told you, he is not well educated, and requires a degree of supervision.[39]

This statement represents Cornelia's personnel management, demonstrating knowledge of men and cattle. It also shows both her judgment and her restraint in terms of finding and retaining good help. Cornelia's comments on Kent would shortly thereafter be tested.

Cornelia additionally explained the land's mortgage situation in some detail; it was because of Hobart's experience in management and sale of land that Cornelia had sought to hire him. It is evident that she knew why and how the debt was incurred—going back to 1885— and how she expected that it would be dispatched, relating land prices, interest rates, and other figures. She also explained the prohibitions on drinking and gambling that had become part of JA tradition under Goodnight's management. It is immediately obvious that Mrs. Adair had not hired a general manager to bail out a sinking ship. Rather, she had hired one to better enact her policies and carry out her vision.

Cornelia Adair was aware of traditional gender roles when she handled her affairs. In the course of explaining one of James Wadsworth Jr.'s unfavorable land deals during his earlier tenure as JA manager, she complained to Hobart, "My nephew was rather a disappointment to me as he inherited from his father the belief that women knew nothing of business and never could be taught anything, and that it was not necessary to consult them about anything." While men of her own family had demonstrated chauvinism, in her second marriage she had become accustomed to something more like a partnership: "my husband was so different and always told me all the details of the business affairs both of the ranch and of his Irish property where he was his own agent and always took me with him when he went to collect his rents etc." She was clearly proud of her own business success in the face of low expectations, remarking, "I do give myself a little credit for having kept that splendid Texas property together through all vicissitudes, when I was often advised to get out of the whole thing."[40] It is clear that Cornelia resented men who would exclude her from her role as owner of the JA because she was a woman.

She was also adept at using gender to her favor. When oil prospectors wished to lease lands on the JA in 1919, she realized that stalling the lease would allow her to avoid extremely high British tax provisions during wartime. She covered her economic motives by playing on American male prejudice, telling Hobart, "To anyone who enquired would it not be as well to say that I am reserving my decision till I come out in the autumn. That will stave off people for the present without annoying them, the worst they can think is that I am rather unreasonable, and I think Americans always expect a woman to be rather unreasonable anyway!"[41] Turnabout was fair play in her world of business; if she was treated with prejudice as a woman by chauvinistic men, she was perfectly capable of using their chauvinism to her advantage.

Cornelia, however, was not necessarily pro-woman, particularly when it came to ranch affairs. She preferred single men as employees rather than men with wives and families. This seemed not only a matter of expense but also of maintaining harmony. Such a hiring practice was not always possible, as the Great War brought labor shortages that required compromises. Cornelia allowed married men at the camps but did not "want too many wives about Headquarters," saying "sometimes they do not always agree."[42] Cornelia often expressed a protective attitude toward some ranch employees, as in the case of her wagon boss, whose wife left him and took their small child with her. When the woman wanted to reconcile with her husband a few months later, Mrs. Adair opposed the idea, saying he "should not bring back that dreadful woman" to the ranch, especially to headquarters. Eventually, she allowed the couple to occupy a camp house miles away from headquarters, and she even bought them a new cook stove.[43] Also along the same vein, after Dick Walsh's marriage it was apparently a problem with Mrs. Walsh "fitting in" with the ranch culture that led to Dick Walsh's departure, ultimately to Rhodesia, in 1910—Cornelia having arranged his position, through her numerous relationships with Lord Kitchener and others, as head of ranches for the British South Africa Company.[44]

Cornelia did not hesitate to alter procedures when she saw opportunities for improvement, even intervening in the almost sacred Texas tradition of men working cattle. One concern involved personnel, the cattle count, and possible cattle theft. This aptly demonstrates Cornelia's overall command of the ranch—its men, its cattle, and its operations— and her management style of patience, tact, and loyalty during J. W. Kent's time as manager.

In the fall of 1915, Cornelia expressed interest in the cattle count, the first under Hobart's management. She had informed him in July that she was concerned with the casual approach that had predominated over "the last few years": "It is difficult to get the old-time cowman to realise the importance of an accurate count in view of the very high price of cattle."[45] Confirming her fears and demonstrating the need for reform, Hobart replied, "There seems to be quite a discrepancy between the recent count of the cattle in the separate pasture as compared with the books. I suppose this might be accounted for in part by small losses of last winter, but I shall hope to make the count very thoroughly another season. I think some improvement may be made in regard to the manner of determining the exact number of steer and heifer calves at branding."[46]

In response, Cornelia was adamant that policies be instituted to ensure an accurate tally moving forward—"cattle are too valuable now to have any discrepancy." She indicated that she had at an earlier time invested in fencing her range into smaller pastures so "if 1,000 cows were given to the care of a man in any of the camps, that man should account for all of them in some way, either their skins if dead should be given up, or some reason given as to why the cows were not there."[47] Cornelia continued to advocate for tighter pastures and increased individual accountability.

Neither explanations nor reforms came speedily enough. In letters to both Kent and Hobart it is evident that Cornelia's patience had run out by the beginning of September, although her tact had not. She explained to Kent, "I have been studying and trying very hard to understand the distribution of the cattle and to make it agree in numbers with the yearly report of the 30th November, but so far as I have gone it seems very difficult. . . . Can you tell me how you account for these differences." She continued to press with specific questions: "Was there any shortage amongst the cows from the Mallard place when they were brought to the Battle Creek?" Her displeasure and her insistence on answers are clear despite her signal of good intentions: "I am sure you will understand that I say all this not from any wish to find fault, but simply to get at the exact figures."[48]

She then wrote Hobart in an even more frank manner that demonstrates her understanding of the problem and its basis in the preceding administrations of the ranch:

> It seems to me absolute folly to have that large herd of very valuable cattle and not have much more carefully looked after [them] now that their value had doubled. Mr. Kent was by way of counting the cattle before having the count entered in to the tally book last year, but Mr. Wadsworth thought that his count had better not be entered as he was sure there were more cattle in the herd than Mr. Kent had counted. . . . I do not see why, now that the Ranch is divided into these comparatively small pastures, the exact number in each pasture could not be ascertained. If it can be proved that it is impossible, I am open to conviction, and would like to have the pastures further divided. I know in Mr. Reynolds' time, in Mr.

Wadsworth's absences, it was awfully carelessly managed, but I am sure we shall be able to arrange differently. It was not worthwhile grading up the cattle as Mr. Walsh did, and buying these most expensive bulls, only to see the herd very much reduced.[49]

Hobart told Cornelia that he had talked with Kent, who had reasoned that the previous year's losses were only a small fraction of the herd and that calculations had not yet been made for the previous winter. As he criticized Kent, Hobart credited Cornelia's plan for smaller pastures as valuable, concluding in part that the size of the range was indeed a challenge to maintaining accuracy.[50]

Hobart's letters reflect the similarity in his and Cornelia's management style and their commitment to solve problems rather than assign blame for past actions. On October 11, from Rathdaire Cottage in Queens County, Ireland, Cornelia wrote:

> **In strict confidence**—of course I consider that there was some cattle-stealing going on in Reynolds' time which might account for some of the discrepancies in the tally and I am sure that if I had not insisted upon his leaving in the middle of the winter of 1913–14 that the discrepancies would have been much greater. However, there is no use referring to that now, and there is nothing to be done except—as you say—to take an accurate count next year which will be much facilitated by the smaller pastures and then to adjust the book to the actual count. I am glad that you agree with me that it will be easier to count in smaller pastures. It seemed to me to be an absolutely necessary change. Of course they mean more careful management and therefore more expense and more men, but this I expect and think the high quality and price of the cattle warrant it.[51]

It was not surprising that Cornelia counseled discretion and favored moving on during her nephew's senatorial administration. It was perhaps in Cornelia's mind that she had pressured Wadsworth to take the job, partially by assuring him that he could manage the JA through periodic visits. Irrespective of family concerns, however, the letter demonstrates again Cornelia's understanding of the situation and pragmatism in moving forward. Moreover, she remains admirably loyal to

Kent, whom she had once dismissed but whom she had come to trust.

Out of this unpleasant matter, management of the JA improved. Cornelia expressed pleasure at the 1915 end-of-year manager's report, which indicated that the "total number of calves branded for the year, including the Hereford and Shorthorn herds, is 8,667—1,984 in excess of the calf crop of 1914."[52] She applauded Hobart's purchase of new Hereford bulls, remarking that she never liked Shorthorns because the climate did not suit them. She also expressed to Hobart that she had consistently told Walsh that the ranch should stock purebred Herefords.[53] This is interesting, as Walsh is typically credited with producing the award-winning Hereford herd. By December 1916, Cornelia expressed satisfaction with the system of fencing and counting: the latest count had exceeded the book estimate. She wrote to Hobart in May 1917, "I am so pleased that I made up my mind to do that dividing up of pastures. I think it will make a sort of friendly competition between the different camp men as to who can have the least loss."[54] The vision of camp men in charge of small pastures was far from the idea of cowboys on the vast space of the JA, a newer way of managing cowboys and cattle that accorded with contemporary corporate models rather than the older, less efficient, methods of earlier times.

Cornelia's privileged position as a Wadsworth meant the luxury of living as she was accustomed. Even as she had told Hobart in March 1915 that she did not wish to treat the JA and land sale operations as her source of capital, when times were tight, she did just that.[55] When her son Jack's illness prescribed a move to southern England for the winter in November 1915, she wrote to Hobart, "I hope you will be able to sell some land for me this winter, as I feel that my finances will require it."[56] Clearly the JA operated in the red during Cornelia's period of ownership. In fairness, however, it is equally clear that she assumed ownership of the ranch already with $350,000 of debt.

The JA's debt was soon to be transferred from primarily family investors to the Union Trust Company of New York.[57] Even as Cornelia paid off former debts, she incurred new ones, borrowing from family and associates with the JA as surety. Cornelia told Hobart that the JA owed $100,000 to the Texas Land and Mortgage Company, $100,000 incurred when Goodnight bought an expensive herd of 5,000 cows and calves in 1885. However, in a rare oversight on her part, records of the Texas Land and Mortgage Company suggest that the loan, which had been in negotiation by John Adair prior to his death, was for much more. In 1885, TLMC's Texas manager Courtenay E. Wellesley cabled, "Board authorizes $300,000, Palo Duro, $50,000 Quitaque. Both first mortgages, both including cattle. Mrs. Adair personally responsible both cases, endorsing $50,000 note also." Historian W. G. Kerr noted that this loan, at 10 percent, "was the largest loan ever advanced by a British mortgage company to an American ranching venture in Texas."[58] At the time of her death, there was still debt of $300,000 in outstanding bank loans and an overall total of more than $750,000 including taxes in both Britain and America.[59] Instructions in her will state that the sale of the JA was to settle her debts and provide for her heirs.

Cornelia faced her last years with no illusions. She spoke frankly of managing the ranch in such a way as to settle affairs to the degree possible. She wanted to clarify her land boundaries and to sell certain parcels of land when financially advantageous and not crucial to JA operations. She also clearly expressed the desire to have her affairs in order so that executors of her estate would not face a horribly complex settlement. Yet she could not bring herself to sell the ranch, though she flirted with the idea regularly. It had become too much a part of her. When away, she wrote, "I never can have too many letters from the Ranch. I am always anxious to hear every detail concerning the employees, the people, the land, and the herds, and if I get a long letter every day in the year it would never be too much."[60] In 1920, she commented, "I am just longing to get back to the ranch, I feel as if that were my real home."[61]

Admittedly, Cornelia was a child of privilege who took her privilege for granted, yet she undertook many good works. Too little credit is given her for her role in philanthropy and regional development,— credit that would have been more easily and fully accorded a man. Cornelia had a vision for development of the Texas Panhandle. She contributed funds for the construction of the Adair Hospital and the YMCA center in Clarendon, the community just to the north of the ranch, and also contributed financially to the Clarendon Episcopal

Church.[62] In a 1912 letter to her Dallas lawyer, Henry Coke, Cornelia expressed her interest in the budding Boy Scout movement and arranged to pay for a scout troop to take the train from Dallas to spend a fortnight camped in the Palo Duro Canyon on JA lands—"Don't you think they would like this?" she asked. Collectively, her gifts in the Panhandle suggest a philanthropic vision of establishing and strengthening social institutions concerning health care, religion, and education. These were only some of her charitable works and say nothing about her substantial philanthropy in Ireland.

As a land manager, she sought to sell land to those who would develop farms, believing—as most did—that agriculture was the natural and desirable path of economic development. She was mindful of areas that she thought would make good town sites, understanding that ranchland would eventually give way to a countryside dotted with municipalities. She had no expectation that the ranch could be sustained, making intent of sale explicit in her will. In her view, the sale of her ranch would settle her debts and provide for her heirs, but the land—held in trust for the future—would give way to progress. In the era of the big Panhandle ranches, she was, as M. K. Brown put it, "an all-around good scout and a real Queen of the Cattle Country."[63]

Cornelia's last known letter is, predictably, to the ranch, and it is a fitting place to conclude. Written from London on September 10, 1921, to her old JA range foreman J. W. Kent, a frail-seeming Cornelia expressed great sorrow at the recent news of Dick Walsh's death in Rhodesia, where he had continued as ranch manager for the British South Africa Company. She reported a recent visit from Vere Finch, member of the British peerage and a neighbor landowner in Texas, who had pleased her by reporting that conditions of the range and cattle were "splendid" in the Panhandle, from whence he had just returned. Still, she was concerned at reports of poor financial conditions and a low price for steers. She informed Kent that she would soon to move to her new house in Bath: "I am going to spend a quiet winter there, trying to get as strong as I can so that I may be able to come back to my beloved ranch and all my friends who I miss so much. I will write again very soon, and remember, I can never hear too often."[64] Cornelia did not manage this final visit, as she died just twelve days later, in Bath on

September 22, 1921. The next spring Hobart wrote, "She frequently expressed a desire that her last resting place might be in the little cemetery near the headquarters."[65] Yet the Queen of the Cattle Country's remains are interred in the wall of Rathdaire Church, County Laois, Ireland, which she had built in 1887 in honor of her late husband and father-in-law.[66] Thereby are the green hills of Ireland forever linked to the Palo Duro pastures of the great JA Ranch.

Without Cornelia Adair's strong engagement with ranch affairs, the JA would certainly not exist today. Had Charles Goodnight had his way, the ranch would have been sold prior to his departure. T. D. Hobart too would probably have succeeded in selling the ranch if not for Cornelia's reluctance. Given Cornelia's era, social position, and life abroad, it would have been typical and expected of her to put the ranch in the hands of a trusted male advisor like Thomas Renshaw or James W. Wadsworth Jr., who would have overseen ranch managers from afar. In this scenario too the ranch might well have been sold or possibly suffered fatally from the neglect of absentee management. Beyond the simple matter of her ownership, Cornelia's constant communication, her insistence that questions of management involve her knowledge and approval, had much to do with the success of the JA Ranch. One can readily imagine that JA managers did not always appreciate Cornelia's communiqués. This perception of micromanagement from abroad may contribute—along with her class privilege and pretension —to the region's people holding her at arm's length as the "English cattle queen" in contrast to the much-loved Molly Goodnight, often regarded as the motherly ranch woman archetype of the Panhandle. Nevertheless, in taking control of her own life and claiming agency in her own complex business affairs, Cornelia Wadsworth Ritchie Adair deserves serious study and respect within Texas ranch culture.

Notes

1. "Beverly Briefs," *Stayer* (Canyon City, Tex.), October 17, 1901.

2. "Beverly Briefs," *Stayer* (Canyon City, Tex.), November 14, 1901.

3. Montagu K. Brown, introduction to Cornelia Adair, *My Diary: August 30th to November 5th, 1874* (Austin: University of Texas Press, 1965), xxiv.

4. Adair, *My Diary*, 118.

5. As Cornelia explained, the journey was facilitated by General Philip Henry Sheridan, Colonel Richard Irving Dodge, and General Henry Andrew Morrow, all of whom knew the Wadsworths. Sheridan knew Cornelia's father, and her brother Craig was on Sheridan's staff in the war. Sheridan arranged for Dodge to guide their trip. Morrow, who was stationed at Sydney, Nebraska, had been a junior officer to General Wadsworth at the Battle of the Wilderness, where Wadsworth had suffered his fatal wound. These connections would also come into play when Cornelia and her husband visited the JA for the first time in 1877. Adair, *My Diary*, 24–25, 68–69. See also Harley True Burton, *A History of the JA Ranch* (New York: Argonaut Press, 1966), 21–22, 31–32n.

6. Ibid., 70, 87.

7. Ibid., 97.

8. Montgomery Ritchie, "Centennial Party," unpublished manuscript, July 9, 1976. Southwest Collection, JA Papers, box 123, folder 35, Texas Tech University, Lubbock, Texas.

9. Burton, *History of the JA Ranch*, 32n.

10. Francis B. Vick, "Cornelia Wadsworth Ritchie Adair," *Texas Women on the Cattle Trails*, ed. Sara R. Massey (College Station: Texas A&M Press, 2006), 159.

11. Burton, *History of the JA Ranch*, 59.

12. Ibid., 61–62.

13. Ibid., 67, 74. According to JA management, today the ranch sells or feeds its calves. If it sells them, it does so after weaning for at least sixty days at about nine months of age.

14. Ibid., 60.

15. H. Allen Anderson, "JA Ranch," *Handbook of Texas Online*, http://www.tshaonline.org/handbook/online/articles/apj01.

16. W. G. Kerr, *Scottish Capital on the American Credit Frontier* (Austin: Texas State Historical Association, 1976), 65–67.

17. Ibid., 76.

18. Burton, *History of the JA Ranch*, 109–10, 119.

19. J. Evetts Haley, *Charles Goodnight: Cowman and Plainsman* (Norman: University of Oklahoma Press, 1949), 354.

20. Such visits are documented for 1891, 1901, 1903, 1909, 1910, 1911, 1914, 1916, 1919, and 1920. However, trace evidence suggests that there were more visits than can be definitely established.

21. Haley, *Charles Goodnight*, 355.

22. Burton, *History of the JA Ranch*, 46.

23. Ibid.

24. Haley, *Charles Goodnight*, 331.

25. Ibid., 332–33.

26. William T. Hagan, *Charles Goodnight: Father of the Texas Panhandle* (Norman: University of Oklahoma Press, 2007), 96.

27. Cornelia Adair to T. D. Hobart, September 5, 1915. T. D. Hobart Papers, Panhandle-Plains Historical Museum Research Center, Canyon, Texas (hereafter PPHM).

28. George F. Walker to Cornelia Adair, October 6, 1892, JA Letterpress Copybook, 1891–1892, JA Ranch Papers, box 2, PPHM.

29. James Cox, *Historical and Biographical Record of the Cattle Industry and the Cattlemen of Texas and Adjacent Territory* (St. Louis: Woodward and Tiernan Printing, 1894), 476.

30. T. D. Hobart, "The JA Ranch," *Producer: The National Live Stock Monthly* 3, no. 11 (1922): 8.

31. Walsh to Adair, April 1896, JA Letterbook 1892, 519–22, PPHM.

32. Cornelia Adair to James W. Wadsworth, December 31, 1910, box 40, 1902–1914, Wadsworth Collection, Library of Congress, Washington, DC (hereafter WCLOC).

33. James W. Wadsworth to Marie Wadsworth, January 17, 1911, box 40, 1902–1914, WCLOC.

34. James W. Wadsworth Jr. to James W. Wadsworth Sr., February 12, 1911, box 40, 1902–1914, WCLOC.

35. James W. Wadsworth Jr. to Alice Wadsworth, 1911, box 7, Family Papers, 1911, WCLOC.

36. Stuart Symington Jr., *Tagging Along: Memories of My Grandfather, James Wolcott Wadsworth, Jr.* (Geneseo, N.Y.: Milne Library, SUNY Geneseo, 2013), 62.

37. L. F. Sheffy, *The Life and Times of Timothy Dwight Hobart: Colonization of West Texas* (Canyon, Tex.: Panhandle-Plains Historical Society, 1950), 197.

38. Cornelia Adair to T. D. Hobart, March 19, 1915, T. D. Hobart Papers, PPHM.

39. Ibid.

40. Adair to Hobart, April 19, 1918, T. D. Hobart Papers, PPHM.

41. Adair to Hobart, February 27, 1919, T. D. Hobart Papers, PPHM.

42. Adair to Hobart, March 20, 1918, T. D. Hobart Papers, PPHM.

43. Ibid.

44. Brown, introduction to Adair, *My Diary*, xviii.

45. Adair to Hobart, July 6, 1915, T. D. Hobart Papers, PPHM.

46. Hobart to Adair, August 7, 1915, T. D. Hobart Papers, PPHM.

47. Adair to Hobart, August 26, 1915, T. D. Hobart Papers, PPHM.

48. Adair to Kent, August 31, 1916, T. D. Hobart Papers, PPHM.

49. Adair to Hobart, September 5, 1915, T. D. Hobart Papers, PPHM.

50. Hobart to Adair, September 25, 1915, T. D. Hobart Papers, PPHM.

51. Adair to Hobart, October 11, 1915, T. D. Hobart Papers, PPHM.

52. "Manager's Report for 1915," T. D. Hobart Papers, PPHM.

53. Adair to Hobart, September 19, 1916, T. D. Hobart Papers, PPHM.

54. Adair to Hobart, May 21, 1917, T. D. Hobart Papers, PPHM.

55. Adair to Hobart, March 19, 1915, T. D. Hobart Papers, PPHM.

56. Adair to Hobart, November 18, 1915, T. D. Hobart Papers, PPHM.

57. Adair to Hobart, March 19, 1915, T. D. Hobart Papers, PPHM.

58. Quoted in W. G. Kerr, *Scottish Capital on the American Credit Frontier* (Austin: Texas State Historical Association, 1976), 75.

59. Freshfields & Leese of London to Henry Coke, September 29, 1921, T. D. Hobart Papers, PPHM.

60. Adair to Hobart, January 2, 1917, T. D. Hobart Papers, PPHM.

61. Adair to Hobart, May 6, 1920, T. D. Hobart Papers, PPHM.

62. Nancy Baker Jones, "Cornelia Wadsworth Adair," *Handbook of Texas Online*, http://www.tshaonline.org/handbook/online/articles/fad02.

63. Brown, introduction to Adair, *My Diary*, xv.

64. Cornelia Adair to J. W. Kent, Kent Papers, PPHM.

65. T. D. Hobart, "The JA Ranch," *Producer: The National Live Stock Monthly* 3, no. 11 (April 1922), 8.

66. W. E. Vaughan, *Sin, Sheep, and Scotsmen: John George Adair and the Derry–veagh Evictions, 1861* (Belfast: Ireland, Appletree Press, 1983), 66–67.

Chapter 4

Mary Jane Alexander
"The First Woman Rancher in the Panhandle"

Jean Stuntz

In May 1962, long after her death in 1929, an Amarillo paper proclaimed Mary Jane Alexander as the first woman rancher in the Panhandle.[1] The success of the Alexander Ranch at that time was due largely to the actions of her son R. T. and successive generations of Alexanders. In 1991 the Alexander Ranch was honored by the Texas Land Heritage organization of the Texas Department of Agriculture for being the oldest continuously operating family-owned ranch in Hemphill County.[2] But who was Mary Jane Alexander? How did she come to ranch in the Texas Panhandle? Was she really the first woman rancher of the Panhandle?

Mary Jane Alexander certainly never set out to be the first women rancher in the Texas Panhandle. Born Mary Jane Mathes on September 3, 1840, in Washington County, Tennessee, she grew up in a staunchly Presbyterian family. Her father was a minister. It was the custom in her family for the eldest son to become a Presbyterian minister, and, if possible, the girls would marry a Presbyterian minister. Mary Jane made her profession of faith earlier than most and was devoted to her religion her whole life. She studied theology, Greek, and Latin so she could be helpful to her future husband. She was self-taught but extremely knowledgeable in the catechisms and dogma of the Presbyterian Church.[3]

Clifton Wrenshaw Alexander was born October 5, 1838, in Jefferson County, Tennessee. He attended Princeton Theological Seminary from 1863 to 1866 and was ordained on his twenty-ninth birthday. Less than a year later, he married Mary Jane Mathes on September 25, 1868. C. W., or Wren, as his family called him, served in several posts before being sent to Texas to teach at Austin College in Sherman. In 1884 the Home Mission Board of the Presbyterian Church (USA) sent him to start a church in the Wild West town of Mobeetie in the eastern Texas Panhandle. He left his wife and children in Sherman while he set up a home for them in Mobeetie.[4]

The next spring Alexander went to fetch his family from Sherman. On the way to Mobeetie, the family came to a raging river. Most of the time the Pease River is dry, with maybe a few puddles of water, but when the spring rains are heavy, as they were in 1885, the river floods. When the horses started across, they got into some quicksand, causing the buggy to start swaying. As they approached the middle of the river, some brush, or maybe a small tree, came rushing down the river and crashed into the side of the buggy. Reverend Alexander was thrown out of the buggy into the river. He went completely underwater for a while and then managed to grab hold of the harness. Mary Jane had been sitting on the front bench holding their baby. She was also thrown into the water but managed to grab the tongue of the buggy and keep her head and her baby's head above water. The horses finally took them safely to the other side. Later they ran into a bad storm, with winds so high that the buggy was lifted off the ground, with them all in it. Everyone got out, and Reverend Alexander staked the buggy down and held on to the ropes. The family sheltered under it until the storm, and possibly a tornado, passed. The family finally arrived in Mobeetie and settled into the only empty house in the town.[5]

Mobeetie was not the kind of place one might imagine such a religious family to inhabit. The first town in the Panhandle created and settled by Anglos, it began as Hide Town, a place where buffalo hunters could stretch and dry their hides in a curve of what they called Sweetwater Creek. The hides were then taken by wagon to the railhead in Kansas. After driving the Comanches onto reservations in Indian Territory after the Red River War, the army established Fort Elliott by the border of Texas and what would become Oklahoma, just east of Hide Town. Merchants arrived to take advantage of the soldiers stationed at the fort, and a town grew up quickly at the site. Most residents, including card dealers, dance hall girls, and prostitutes, made their living off the soldiers' paychecks. "Probably many of the less respectable population were more rowdy than mean," one Panhandle historian writes. Regardless of makeup, the town housed people who sent requests to a variety of denominations for new churches and preachers, and the Presbyterian Church sent Reverend Alexander.[6]

But this story does not focus on Wren Alexander. When he had fallen into the raging Pease River, his lungs had filled with water, and subsequently an unknown contagion festered in his respiratory system. A few months later he was caught in a rainstorm as he was riding his circuit. Drenched and chilled, he caught pneumonia and died, leaving Mary Jane with five children in a lawless town with no other family and few friends. Most widows at that time remarried soon to support their families, but Mary Jane did not. Another option was to move back east and live with family, but Mary Jane did not do that either. Instead she homesteaded on one section of land in Hemphill County and bought the adjoining section. She ordered lumber to be sent by rail to Harrold, a small city to the south, then delivered by wagon to her land and had a two-room half-dugout built near the creek that ran through the property. This house became a beacon for travelers in the area.[7]

The first years on the ranch were extremely difficult. Alexander and her children found ways to make money needed to buy supplies. The children gathered wild grasses growing on the prairie, bundled it, and sold it to the soldiers in Fort Elliott for livestock fodder. When buffalo hunters had been in the area a few years earlier, they had tended to slaughter and skin the buffalos and leave most of the meat and bones where they lay. Once carrion eaters and nature had their way, over the years large piles of buffalo bones remained. The children gathered these too, and the second son, R. T., who was then fourteen, transported the bones in a wagon from Canadian, Texas, to Dodge City, Kansas, and sold them for use in making fertilizer. After the bones were all gone, young R. T. continued to carry freight from Mobeetie to Kansas and back.[8]

Mary Jane did many things to bring in money for her family. She served as postmaster for the small town of Cataline near her ranch. Her girls, who were given the opportunity to name the town, named it for the famous Roman senator because they were studying Roman history—or after the cat they had named for the famous Roman. Mary Jane served as Cataline's postmaster from September 4, 1893, to August 28, 1899. Her son R. T. then assumed the position until July 12, 1900.[9]

Mary Jane took advantage of opportunity when it presented itself. She gathered sand plums that grew wild along the creek; while these were not good for eating, they made an excellent jelly. She made her

Figure 7. Mary Jane Alexander. Courtesy of Panhandle-Plains Historical Museum Research Center.

own gelatin by boiling beef bones and could buy sugar in town, but she still needed jelly jars. The only way to get anything to the Panhandle was by wagon, and jelly jars did not provide high enough profit to justify shipping them, so Mary Jane had to be inventive. She went to Mobeetie in the mornings or early afternoons when the saloons were quiet and gathered bottles that had been tossed out behind the tents. She brought the bottles home and cleaned them, then soaked string in kerosene, tied it around the bottles, and set it on fire. As soon as it burned out, she dropped each bottle into a bucket of water, and the top would crack off, leaving a jar for her jelly.[10]

Mary Jane encouraged her sons to ride around the area looking for unbranded cattle, and there were a lot of wild longhorns in those days. Her sons branded the animals and brought them onto her sections, which began the Alexander herd. As R. T. grew up, he learned about scientifically improving herds and began buying Hereford cattle, first to interbreed with the longhorns and then to replace them altogether. His breeding program produced one of the finest Hereford herds in the state, maybe in the country. R. T. took over in 1895, but it was Mary Jane who owned the ranch and ran it from 1886 to 1895, making it possible for others to give her the title of first woman rancher in the Panhandle.[11]

She worked hard at being a good rancher. Though the tax rolls show her with only one cow in 1887, she had twenty-three in 1888, forty in 1890, and eighty in 1892. Her brother-in-law delivered prized cattle in exchange for paying railroad shipping charges, and this quality stock eventually improved her herd. By the time R. T bought the ranch, there were 125 head valued at almost $1,000. In 1887 Mary Jane had the ranch fenced in with used barbed wire from Sayre, Oklahoma. Although most reports say that Mary Jane lived on the ranch for twenty years, the US Census of 1900 shows her living in a rented house with her three youngest children in the small town of Leonard, in Fannin County, Texas, well over three hundred miles southeast of Mobeetie. Until 1904, daughters Lucy and Nona taught at the new Leonard Collegiate Institute founded in 1898. Mary Jane came back to the ranch and lived there until 1906, and then moved to Canadian to live with daughter Nona and family.[12]

Figure 8. Mary Jane Alexander and family. Courtesy of Panhandle-Plains Historical Museum Research Center.

Her day-to-day life was not exciting, unless it was a day when Comanches came over from the reservation hoping to get some free food and maybe have some fun at the expense of whites. They came into her house uninvited, looked through everything, sometimes taking some of her jelly, sometimes trading for beads and other trinkets. Mary Jane generally rose early, made breakfast, did her chores, said her prayers, and just did whatever needed doing. Sundays were days of rest and worship only—no other work was done except for necessary tasks. Most food was prepared on Saturday, which was also when church clothes were laid out and boots were polished. She did make one exception to the no-work-on-Sunday rule. One time a neighbor rode up on a Sunday morning and asked her to come to his house to take care of him and his family who had all become sick. She saddled up and went to take care of her neighbors. Mercy and necessity were the only exceptions to the rule.[13]

Mary Jane excelled as a pioneer woman and a ranch woman. She raised her children well, educating them in reading, writing, arithmetic, and Presbyterian theology. She had all her children educated at Park College in Missouri. When her daughters Nona and Lucy attended college, she went with them to serve as housemother. Lucy earned advanced degrees and became a missionary in China. Nona became a teacher until she married. The eldest son, Hugh, became a Presbyterian minister, as was family tradition. R. T. took over the ranch operations. Youngest son Erastus became a physician in New York. Her other children, Allis, born in 1877, John C., born in 1879, and Maude and John Bunyan, born between 1883 and 1885, did not survive to adulthood.[14]

Mary Jane excelled at homemaking. She could make delicious biscuits—from scratch, of course—on a wood stove. Once, when she went to nurse a sick neighbor, she came home to find that the children had tried to make biscuits for company but had used the wrong ingredients. Mary Jane made a new batch in fifteen minutes, and the company never knew. She could put out a chimney fire without panicking by organizing the children into a bucket brigade. She provided medical services to people all over the area and could be inventive when necessary. Mary Jane saved her son Erastus from bleeding to death by putting flour on the hand he injured while exploding shotgun shells. She was also renowned for her hospitality. Her small house was a stopover spot for travelers. No matter who they were, they received a place to sleep and good food. During one snowstorm, so many people ended up at her house that all the men had to go sleep in the barn while the women and children slept all over the house. That crowd depleted her food supplies, so everyone pitched in what they had. She adopted children escaping from abusive situations and did her best to train them in her own upright ways.[15]

Mary Jane lived the life she had trained for, that of a Christian and minister's wife. While her husband was still alive, she served with him in the churches, organizing Sunday schools and doing all the unrecognized jobs that any minister's wife does. After he died and she moved to the ranch, she organized the first Sunday school in Hemphill County. She had Bible readings for her children and any guests who stayed overnight. She went to church every Sunday unless she was caring for someone. Mary Jane was known for her piety and Christian charity, her kindness, and her generosity.[16]

Cowboys who worked on the ranch and on the larger ranches nearby looked to her as a motherly figure, someone who commanded respect. They helped her any time they heard she needed it, and she was beloved by all. This is said of a lot of people after they die, but in this case it seems to have been true. As she neared death in 1929, word spread. People who had known her throughout her life came to Canadian to visit with her one last time. Hundreds of people, some who had stayed the night at her house, some who had worked for her, some who had gone to church with her, and some who had known her at Park College, came to say goodbye.[17]

Her life represents the lives of many pioneer women who scraped by, did their best, and put their faith in God. Mary Jane raised her five children to be fine, upstanding adults. She was a success in every aspect of her life. In 1963 managers of the Panhandle-Plains Historical Museum in Canyon were fund-raising to expand their building. R. T. gave $5,000 to fund a gallery space named for Reverend C. W. and Mary Jane Alexander, and it was always to have exhibits that honored Panhandle pioneers. That gallery still exists and honors those pioneers.[18]

Mary Jane Alexander deserves recognition as one of the pioneers of the Panhandle, but was she truly the first women rancher? She was not the first Anglo woman to live on a ranch in the Panhandle. All the large ranches had ranch managers who were usually married men. Mary Ann "Molly" Goodnight of the JA Ranch in Randall County and Mrs. W. W. Wetsel of the Frying Pan Ranch in Potter County are two of the Anglo women known to have lived on Panhandle ranches before 1886. Other women, even in the eastern Panhandle, owned horses and cattle. Tax records for Hemphill County from 1889 show Mrs. M. J. Riddle with six horses and nine head of cattle, Mrs. E. F. Turner with thirty head of cattle, Mrs. E. J. Wood with two horses and thirteen head of cattle, and Mrs. E. M. Wilson with eighteen horses and fifty head of cattle.[19] Wheeler County tax records show Mary Jane owning two horses and ten head of cattle in 1887, although the Hemphill County records show just one cow.[20] Is that enough to qualify as a ranching operation? Does this make her the first woman rancher of the Panhandle?

The answer depends, to a large extent, on the definition of "rancher." If a rancher is someone who owns land with a few cattle, and the land later expands into a ranch, then, yes, Mary Jane would be the first in Hemphill County. If the definition is someone who makes the majority of one's income from the selling of cattle, then she would not be the first, since the Alexanders' income did not depend on cattle while she owned the land. There is no record of how actively involved she was in the running of the ranch. Even from a young age R. T. seems to have made most of the decisions about buying and selling cattle. One can make both arguments.

Mary Jane Alexander may have been the first woman to own and operate a ranch in the region. But, more importantly, she was a resourceful entrepreneur who did what she could to subsidize and support her family. She would have described herself as a wife or widow, a mother, or as a person of faith instead of calling herself a rancher. Her ownership of the ranch only lasted a few years. When that Amarillo newspaper awarded Mary Jane Alexander the title of first woman rancher in the Panhandle, it praised her for being successful in a man's occupation—no higher praise in 1961. But Mary Jane really excelled in the traditional woman's roles of wife, mother, and caregiver and in being pious, resourceful, and determined to make a good life for her children. That these qualities were overlooked in 1961 says more about the gender expectations of that time than it does about Mary Jane Alexander.

Notes

1. *Amarillo Globe-Times*, May 31, 1962.

2. *Canadian (Tex.) Record*, November 14, 1991.

3. "A Monograph of the Life of Mrs. Mary Jane Alexander: A Tribute of Love from Her Children," unpublished, 1929, Panhandle-Plains Historical Museum Research Center (hereafter PPHMRC), Canyon, Texas.

4. Clifton Wrenshaw Alexander file, PPHMRC; Georgellen Burnett, *We Just Toughed It Out: Women in the Llano Estacado*, Southwestern Studies 90 (El Paso: Texas Western Press, 1990), 111.

5. Millie Jones Porter, *Memory Cups of Panhandle Pioneers* (Clarendon, Tex.: Clarendon Press, 1945), 272.

6. Frederick W. Rathjen, *The Texas Panhandle Frontier*, rev. ed. (Lubbock: Texas Tech University Press, 1998), 132, 182.

7. Burnett, *We Just Toughed It Out*, 22; R. T. Alexander, "Memories of R. T. Alexander as related to C. Boone McClure," May 10, 1958 (PPHMRC); Porter, *Memory Cups*, 272; *Amarillo Globe-Times*, May 31, 1962.

8. Alexander, "Memories of R. T. Alexander"; Porter, *Memory Cups*, 272.

9. Burnett, *We Just Toughed It Out*, 40; Sallie B. Harris, *Cowmen and Ladies: A*

History of Hemphill County (Midland, Tex.: Staked Plains Press, 1977), 149.

10. Burnett, *We Just Toughed It Out*, 22; Alexander, "Memories of R. T. Alexander."

11. *Amarillo Globe-Times*, May 31, 1962; tax rolls, Hemphill County, Texas, 1886–99; Alexander, "Memories of R. T. Alexander."

12. Tom Hymer, *The History of Leonard, Texas*, vol. 2 (Leonard Preservation League, Leonard Chamber of Commerce, n.d.), 26–27; Tax rolls, Hemphill County, 1887–1900; Burnett, *We Just Toughed It Out*, 23; Alexander, "Memories of R. T. Alexander"; *Amarillo Globe-Times*, May 31, 1962.

13. "Monograph of the Life of Mrs. Mary Jane Alexander."

14. Burnett, *We Just Toughed It Out*, 35; US Census, 1900, 1910, 1920.

15. "Monograph of the Life of Mrs. Mary Jane Alexander"; Burnett, *We Just Toughed It Out*, 32–28.

16. Burnett, *We Just Toughed It Out*, 35, 38.

17. Ibid., 35; Sallie B. Harris, *Cowmen and Ladies: A History of Hemphill County* (Canyon, Tex.: Staked Plains Press, 1978.

18. *Amarillo Globe-Times*, May 31, 1962.

19. Tax rolls, Hemphill County, Texas.

20. Tax rolls, Wheeler County, Texas, 1879–1910.

Chapter 5

Mattie B. Morris Miller

Matriarch, Ranch Woman, and Benefactor

Jack Becker

On the first day of 1921, Mattie B. Morris Miller and her two brothers became the proud owners of the Rafter-3 Ranch, in Coleman County, Texas. Their father, J. P. Morris, after several years of careful planning, had placed the vast majority of his ranchland into a trust for his six living children. Mattie B., Claude, and Press Morris each received approximately twelve thousand acres. They pooled their land and about thirty-eight hundred head of cattle to form the Morris Cattle Company.[1]

When Mattie B. and her brothers took over their father's ranch it was one of the largest and best-run commercial Hereford cattle operations in West Texas. When building his ranching operation, J. P. Morris had traded for or purchased several small ranches and farms adjoining the original Clay Mann Ranch and by working hard, spending wisely, living modestly, and paying off debts promptly, Morris was able to leave the ranch to his children relatively debt-free.[2]

Mattie B. and her brothers used the same headquarters as their father had, the former Clay Mann Ranch, ten miles northeast of the city of Coleman, on the banks of Indian Creek approximately a mile west of where it flows into Jim Ned Creek. J. P. Morris had seen the ranch for the first time on a cattle drive in the late 1870s and bought it in 1884. As the oldest child, Mattie B. received the ranch, which later became the home place of the Rafter-3 brand, the brand her father had used in South Texas before he moved to Coleman County.[3] The tradition in which the oldest child of each generation received the home place and the use of the Rafter-3 brand is still followed by Mattie B.'s descendants. As of this writing, 2018, the home place, original ranch, and the brand are owned and used by Julie Shaw, Mattie B.'s great granddaughter.

Mattie B. was born on July 16, 1874, in a three-room house near Hochheim, DeWitt County, Texas, and she eventually became the oldest of the seven children born to J. P. and Martha Miranda Picham Morris, her mother. Like most children born on or near the frontier of Texas, Mattie B. learned the importance of hard work, strong family ties, and love of the land, ranching, and community. Later in life she transmitted these same beliefs to her children and grandchildren, which may explain why the ranch, now known as the Rafter-3, still remains in the family.[4]

The Morris family lived in Coleman, not at the ranch, so Mattie B. and her siblings could attend school. After finishing school in Coleman she attended Baylor College for Females in Belton, Texas, where she became the first person in her family to earn a college degree. After graduation, she planned to become a teacher, but her mother died after a short illness in 1899, and Mattie B. moved back to her father's house and assumed the care of her two youngest siblings, Press and Josephine, aged seven and nine respectively. A year later Mattie B. married J. A. B. Miller, a lawyer, and the new couple remained in her father's home until J. P. remarried in 1904.[5]

Mattie B. and J. A. B. Miller had seven children during their sixteen-year marriage: John P. (Jake) (1900–74), Thomas Louie (1903–63), Claude (1905–76), Mattie B. Rogers (1908–82), Paul (1910–17), Doris Miller (1912–85), and Morris (1914–93). At the age of fifty-one, J. A. B. died suddenly after a short illness, leaving Mattie B. to care for the children who then ranged in age from fourteen years to eight months old. Mattie B. never remarried, and after her husband's death she went to work at her father's ranch office located in Coleman on the corner of Live Oak and Concho Streets. Mattie B. would work in that office for over sixty years, "doing the books"—first for her father, then her brothers, and finally for her own ranching operation. Thus Mattie

Figure 9. Mattie B. Morris Miller with her family in Coleman, Texas. *Left to right*: J. A. B. Miller, John (Jake), Claude, and Mattie B. Courtesy of Southwest Collection/Special Collections Library, Texas Tech University, Lubbock.

B. started her active career in the ranching business soon after her husband's death in 1915.[6]

When Mattie B. and her brothers formed the Morris Cattle Company, Claude, the older of her two brothers, became the foreman and lived at the home place on Indian Creek; Press lived on ranch property in Silver Valley about fifteen miles to the west; and Mattie B. remained in town where she kept the books for the partnership. As with many other families who are in business together, the Morrises' personal, family, and ranch business became mixed.[7]

Mattie B. kept the books for the Morris Cattle Company but also helped her father and brothers with their businesses. At any one time she managed the accounts for at least six different business operations. To keep the accounts separated properly, she first entered each transaction into a daybook and later transferred the transaction into the proper account book. Through the years at least two of her sisters shared the office with her, taking care of their own business operations, which included farming as well as oil and gas leases.[8]

The first year of her partnership with her brothers, 1921, turned out to be a difficult one, as the economic conditions from 1919 to 1932 forced one out of every seven US farmers or ranchers off their land. Ranchers were especially hard hit as cattle prices dropped from a wartime average of $14.50 per hundred pounds in 1918 to an average of only $6.00 per hundred pounds in 1922. Further hampering ranchers' ability to make a living, prices they paid for supplies and labor stayed the same, inflation remained high, beef consumption shrank, and taxes rose. The Morris Cattle Company suffered through this period like all other ranchers did, and for the first three years of its existence it lost money. The company between 1921 and 1923 sold at least $41,000 worth of livestock annually, but high labor costs, low cattle prices, and high taxes kept them in the red. In 1922 the partners tried to make good some losses from the previous year by purchasing cattle, probably steers, for resale. They purchased $67,000 worth of cattle, but it turned out they had bought the cattle on a declining market and lost over $26,000 in 1922 alone. To make matters worse, the company suffered a disastrous fire in the summer of 1923, when lightning struck the ranch headquarters on Indian Creek and burned it to the ground. Built before 1884 by Clay Mann, the building had stood for over forty years and was valued at $15,000. This fire also destroyed over twelve hundred acres of grassland as well as livestock valued at $1,475.[9]

From 1924 until 1929, the Morris Cattle Company began to make a profit as cattle prices rose. In 1924 the siblings spent almost $12,000 on feed, pasture rent, and the unexpected cost of shipping their cow herd to Oklahoma. In periods of dry weather, like 1924, the compa-

ny shipped part or all of their cow herd to Oklahoma or rented pasture elsewhere until rains restored the grasslands of Coleman County.
Each year between 1924 and 1930, Coleman County suffered from
below-average precipitation. The deficit ranged between four and
seven inches each year in an area that normally averaged a little over
twenty-seven inches annually. The accumulated shortfall forced the
partners to look for grass as far away as Ouachita National Forest in
eastern Oklahoma. Morris Cattle Company shipped the cattle to Oklahoma where the herd remained for almost two years, with Press, the
youngest and recently married brother, staying with the herd the entire
time.[10]

Like all ranching operations, the Morrises had significant operating
costs, and the partners fought hard to control them. Most years their
labor costs were their largest operating expense, sometimes reach-
ing over $5,600. The exception was 1926, when they paid more than
$7,900 for grass leases, of which $6,000 went to Dr. E. L. Knox, their
sister Josephine's husband. Leasing grassland or renting pasture was
and remains a common practice in the ranching industry. In a dry year,
like 1926, with a rising cattle market, the company could afford to lease
hundreds of acres of rangeland. This allowed the company to save its
own pastures from overgrazing while holding their herd together. Additionally, the partners could pasture their calves longer and sell them
at heavier weights and at higher prices.[11]

The years from 1926 to 1928 were the best that US cattle producers
experienced following World War I. During this time the Morris Cattle Company prospered, as the expanding US population consumed
more beef and as prices for beef cattle rose to meet demand. In 1926
alone, the company generated over $76,000 in gross income for its
owners, most of it, $70,982, from cattle sales. The company sold cattle
and calves throughout the year, shipping odd allotments of cattle to the
Fort Worth livestock market by truck or rail.[12]

Throughout the twenty-six-year period of their partnership together,
Mattie B. and her brothers operated their ranch as a cow-calf operation,
which generated most of their income from the sale of high-quality
commercial Hereford calves. The calves sold in groups of as many as six
hundred head every fall or spring. It was not an easy process to sell that

many calves and took three days of hard work to accomplish. It took one day to separate the calves from their mothers, another day to drive the calves to shipping pens west of the ranch at Silver Valley, and a third day to load them onto a special train to transport them to the buyer.[13]

The late 1920s became so profitable for the Morris Cattle Company that by 1928 Claude and Press decided to go into a joint cattle-raising operation with a partner, John Buie. Together they formed Morris, Buie, & Morris and in May 1928 purchased the Bluff Creek Ranch in Shackelford County. They stocked their ranch with over a thousand steers and made some minor improvements, all with borrowed money. In hindsight they should not have done this; their timing could not have been worse. In 1929, at the beginning of the Great Depression, the bottom fell out of the livestock market, and the partners had no choice but sell their steers at a loss, which put the partners in a desperate financial situation. Morris, Buie, & Morris made only one payment on the Bluff Creek Ranch. In late 1931 the problems at Bluff Creek threatened to take down not only Bluff Creek Ranch but the Morris Cattle Company too.[14]

In an attempt to make a payment on the Bluff Creek Ranch, Claude and Press mortgaged their two-thirds share of the cattle they owned jointly with Mattie B. in 1931. By early 1932 it became obvious that borrowing against the Morris Cattle Company to pay off the loan on the Bluff Creek Ranch was not going to work, and so, later that same year, their father stepped in to help his children. J. P. devised a plan with Mattie B. to help Claude and Press save their Bluff Creek Ranch without pulling the Morris Cattle Company under.

The plan had Mattie B. mortgaging her one-third share of the Morris Cattle Company herd and giving the money to her brothers. The brothers would then use the proceeds to make a payment on the Bluff Creek Ranch loan. The elder Morris took over the payments of his sons' mortgage on their two-thirds share of the Morris Cattle Company herd. In addition, the elder Morris took over their payments on Bluff Creek and refinanced their loan through the Federal Land Bank. He guaranteed the loan with the mineral rights on Bluff Creek Ranch, which he now owned. The two brothers, besides signing away their mineral rights to Bluff Creek, placed the ranch into a trust administered by Mattie B. and her sisters.[15]

Forming a trust protected Claude and Press from any additional legal or financial problems and allowed them to stay in cattle ranching, working for but not owning the Morris Cattle Company. Claude and Press, along with their partner John Buie, lost their interest in Bluff Creek since they had to sign it and all of their financial obligations over to the elder Morris. This meant Mattie B. owned the Morris Cattle Company along with her father, not her two brothers. Although the terms of the agreement seem harsh, especially for Claude and Press, the agreement made it possible for the family to remain in the cattle business and keep the home place on Indian Creek. By 1935, the Morris Cattle Company was once again in the black. Although cattle prices remained low, Mattie B. and her father had pulled together and weathered the Depression, and the company made a profit every year until the end of World War II.[16]

After her father's death in 1937, Mattie B. became the sole owner of the Morris Cattle Company and co-administrator of the Bluff Creek Ranch, which remained in trust for her brothers. Very little changed in the operation of the company, as her brothers continued the everyday operations of the ranch. This arrangement continued until 1947 when Mattie B. dissolved the Morris Cattle Company because of her brothers' declining health.[17]

Press died in late 1947 after a long struggle with Buerger's disease. Two years later Claude died at the age of seventy-two. Mattie B. took over the management of Bluff Creek along with her sons, who ran the family's day-to-day cattle operations.[18]

When she dissolved the Morris Cattle Company partnership, Mattie B., at the age of seventy-two, created the Rafter-3 Cattle Company with her children. She ran Rafter-3 with her sons just as she had operated the Morris Cattle Company with her two brothers. She remained in town taking care of the books, while her sons Jake and Claude, ran the ranches on Indian Creek and Bluff Creek. At one time or the other, all six of her living children worked for the Rafter-3 Cattle Company. Jake, Mattie B.'s oldest, lived on the home place on Indian Creek, while Claude lived elsewhere on ranch property. Jake's assistance was probably needed to help with family businesses outside of ranching, as the family had extensive gas and oil leases, municipal, state, and school bonds, and banking that had to be managed. Mattie B.'s second-oldest son, Thomas Louie, suffered from poor health and helped in the ranch office while living in Coleman with his family. All of these business interests started by Mattie B.'s father had been left in a trust for his children. Mattie B., as the oldest child, made sure the provisions of the trust were carried out.[19]

It soon became apparent that all family members could not make a living on the ranches in Coleman and Shackelford Counties, so by the early 1950s Claude left the Bluff Creek Ranch and along with his youngest brother, Morris, moved to South Dakota to start ranching operations near Rapid City. For a time, the two brothers experimented with raising sheep, but they quickly returned to cattle-raising. Their move left Jake living at the home place on Indian Creek.[20]

In 1957, in her early eighties, Mattie B. drove herself to South Dakota to visit her sons and their families, stopping along the way to visit relatives. Her trip took her away from home for two and a half weeks. She no doubt wanted to visit her sons, their wives, and her grandchildren, but she also wanted to see her sons' ranching operations in South Dakota. Their South Dakota endeavor remained part of the family's business until the late 1990s.[21]

Under Mattie B.'s management the Rafter-3 Cattle Company remained primarily a commercial cow-calf operation, but the company changed over time in many important ways. When her father bought the ranch in 1884, it appeared little different from the surrounding rangeland. With constant improvements over the years, the ranch became what can best be described as a farm-ranch operation, as the family grew a mixture of cash crops as well as raising livestock. Mattie B. and her sons experimented with raising sheep and ranch horses.[22]

Throughout the 1930s through the 1960s, Mattie B. and her brothers, and then her children, sold the largest part of the ranch's calf crop every fall. In the 1930s she sold the calves to the same buyer, Jim Jett of Emporia, Kansas, who paid four dollars per hundred pounds for steers and three dollars per hundred for heifers. When sold, the calves weighed between 450 and 500 pounds, depending on the available grass. Most years the company held over its smallest calves to sell the following year in the spring.[23]

In years of average or above-average rainfall, Mattie B. ran between two thousand and twenty-four hundred mother cows on the ranch property or one cow-calf pair for every twenty-five to thirty acres. In dry years they ran less, sometimes fewer than two thousand. Every year the ranch kept its biggest and best heifer calves to replace old or nonproductive cows. Holding back heifers maintained the mother cow herd at a desired level. Using registered high-quality bulls and keeping the best heifers improved the quality and assured the quantity of the cow herd. In the fall of every year they culled the old, sick, and barren cows, sometimes up to 20 percent of the herd.[24] The Morris Cattle Company kept between 200 and 400 heifers every year as replacements. If large numbers of replacement cows were needed, up to half of one year's heifer crop could be held back for future cows.[25]

Figure 10. Mattie B. Morris Miller working at the ranch office in Coleman circa 1954. Note the picture of her father beside her on the desk. Courtesy of Southwest Collection/Special Collections Library, Texas Tech University, Lubbock.

From the ranch office Mattie B. planned the breeding program. She knew like most ranchers that "a bull was half the future herd," so she gave much attention to the selection of potential herd sires. She liked to use bulls closely related to each other, often purchasing half-brothers, as she felt bulls related to each other produced calves similar in shape and size and thus more profitable for the ranch. At any one time the Morris Cattle Company owned up to 140 bulls, or one for every fifteen cows, a normal ratio for range conditions like those found in Coleman County. Ranchers turned out a set of bulls every month to six weeks, which meant cows dropped calves year-round. To produce a uniform group of calves, which buyers preferred, Mattie B. managed the cow herd so they all calved about the same time in the fall or spring. The vast majority, however, calved in the spring. Care had to be taken to place enough healthy bulls with the cows, for if they became old, crippled, or infertile, the next year's calf crop suffered.[26]

Mattie B. also selected bulls that "threw" thrifty, fast-growing calves that commercial feedlot operators preferred. Other qualities she looked for in bulls included the birth weight of the calves they sired, their disposition, and soundness of their feet and legs. In some years Mattie B. purchased fifteen bulls at a time, often from the same purebred breeder. She did not, however, "keep the papers up" on the registered Hereford bulls she purchased, stating that she did not have the land to keep two separate herds of cattle properly and register all of the offspring as purebred. As she was not in the purebred business but instead was a commercial cattle operator, she remained content purchasing registered Hereford bulls and raising high-quality Hereford calves.[27]

Throughout the years of the Morris Cattle Company partnership and then the Rafter-3 Cattle Company, Mattie B. worked with her brothers and sons to improve their cattle and protect the rangeland they owned. Changes in the cattle industry and consumer tastes for beef required adaptation. They built fences, dug water tanks, and in many other ways improved their ranch. New and improved fencing made it easier to control grazing and allowed the periodic movement of the cattle to prevent overgrazing. Good fences kept repaired also aided in the breeding program, keeping stray cattle and bulls out of their herd and keeping their registered Hereford bulls at home. Digging new water tanks and improving existing ones insured that the cattle found water to drink no matter where they grazed.[28]

Hired help built many of the improvements on the ranch, and like every other large ranch owner, Mattie B. hired extra help throughout the year. From the office in Coleman, Mattie B. planned the projects, negotiated the hiring of the workers, and then paid them upon completion of the work. Ranch records are filled with notes that her brothers and sons wrote, instructing her how much to pay hands for work. The notes were often written on the back of blank checks or scraps of paper. The wages ranged from fifty cents to almost fifty dollars. She always paid the wages with a check and carefully entered the transaction into the proper daybook and then later transferred the payments to the correct ledger.[29]

During the busy times of the year, usually in the fall and spring, the ranch hired seasonal workers who weighed and moved cattle, worked on water tanks, cooked, and burned prickly pear. In South Texas and West Texas, in periods of drought, the thorns of the prickly pear cactus were burned off so cattle could eat them without getting mouthfuls of stickers. In a job that required mules, such as repairing or building water tanks, a worker earned more money by providing one's own mules. Seasonal hands worked from less than a full day to more than twenty.[30]

Some names appear on ranch records regularly, indicating a ready pool of seasonal workers who could be found in the area. The ranch also apparently regularly hired Mexican and Tejano workers since many Spanish surnames appear on the records. These men received the same wages for the same work as other workers, although their labor was often used for fence construction and repairs. Keeping ranch fences and gates in good condition required constant work. Although full-time employees "rode the fences" and repaired gates on occasion, a great deal of expense went into hiring extra help keeping the fences, gates and corrals in good repair.[31]

There were at least two and probably more full-time employees who lived and worked on the ranch. They earned between $1 and $1.25 daily, depending on their job responsibilities and experience.

Full-time workers did many of the day-to-day, routine jobs that all ranching operations required, including checking on and working with the cattle, repairing fences, and taking care of other ranch livestock. Full-time employees could earn extra money by performing jobs that either required extra skill or were dangerous. In one month Summer McKinnley, a full-time employee, earned an extra fifty dollars breaking ranch horses. Additional money could also be earned by hauling livestock or produce to market.[32]

Although actively running the Morris Cattle Company, which grew an additional twenty-five thousand acres under her management, and raising a large family, Mattie B. found time to participate in many civic projects, which she felt improved the lives of the citizens of Coleman. She volunteered for every philanthropic organization that asked for her help. She worked for the March of Dimes, formed to eradicate infantile paralysis, and the Warm Springs Foundation created to end polio, as well as the American Red Cross and the Coleman Cemetery Association. In addition she served on the Coleman County Board of Education for twelve years, taught Sunday school for over thirty years at the First Presbyterian Church, and sang in the church choir.[33]

Mattie B. also found time for the Colman Public library. Her involvement with the library began with her membership in the Women's Club of Coleman, or the Self-Culture Club, which had supported the library as far back as 1885. The club contributed to the purchase of a building, supplied it with books, and paid the librarian's salary of five dollars per month. The existence of the library became threatened when the librarian quit and no replacement could be found, so in 1921 Mattie B. took over the role of librarian, a job she kept until 1964, when she was ninety years old. For over fifty years she was the sole librarian, cataloger, janitor, reader's advisor to the youth of Coleman County, and purchaser of books. After the county ended its funding, Mattie B. took it upon herself to buy books for the library, although gifts were always welcomed. By 1960 the library contained nearly six thousand books, of which over two thousand circulated annually.[34]

For many years she read every book placed on the shelves of the library in an attempt to insure that no books "[could] inflame the mind" of the youngsters of Coleman County. She especially abhorred "modern fiction—crime novels or cheap fiction." She worked tirelessly to find out the interests of every child who visited the library and made sure they received the books that interested them. She also took special pride in helping children develop an interest in a subject that might later turn into their career.[35]

Toward the end of her life, on July 14, 1961, Mattie B. wrote a brief summary of her life in a daybook while working in the office:

> 87 years ago I was taken into the circle of my mother and father's home and have lived with and among them ever since. It has been a wonderful life, a happy home, lovely associations, with my grandmother, uncles, aunts, and above all a most wonderful mother and father. Then when school and home training were almost over, our mother was stricken with pneumonia and died. I was the big sister to my sisters and brothers. In 1899 October I married a wonderful man, a gentleman, cultured, refined—a civil lawyer and continued to live at home caring for the family. In two years my first baby was born . . . and Papa remarried in 1904. . . . Well it has been a long time but short. [With] five living sons and two daughters left to take care of each other. It has been wonderful having the finest family ever.[36]

Mattie B. died on February 27, 1969, at ninety-four years of age. She was in many ways a remarkable woman who saw many changes in her long and busy life.[37]

As Mattie B.'s life demonstrates, not all successful ranchers in Texas were men, and not all successful ranch women took what might conceivably be called a conventional path to success. Women's roles in the cattle raising industry varied widely, a testament perhaps to their versatility, determination, and desire to better the circumstances of their children. What makes Mattie B.'s life exceptional is the fact that she not only played an active role in the management of the Morris Cattle Company and later the Rafter-3 Cattle Company but also raised a large family and found the time to make a major impact on the culture, education, and religious lives of the people of Coleman County in the early and middle twentieth century.

Notes

This chapter was originally published as "Mattie B. Morris Miller: Matriarch, Ranch Woman, and Benefactor" in *West Texas Historical Association Year Book* 80 (2004): 126–36. Many thanks to the West Texas Historical Association for permission to reprint it in this book.

1. J. P. Morris to his children, January 1, 1921, box 1, folder 3, Morris Ranch Collection, Southwest Collection, Texas Tech University, Lubbock (hereafter MRC); J. P. Morris, contract with Mattie B. Morris Miller, C. A. Morris & Press Morris, December 1, 1920, box 1, folder 5, MRC. Ranch records reveal the use of two names for the ranch Mattie B. and her brothers created—"Morris Cattle Company" and "J. P. Morris Cattle Company." I will use "Morris Cattle Company" for the ranch between the years 1920 and 1947. Mattie B.'s three sisters did not elect to join in the ranching operations.

2. J. P. Morris, Personal Income Tax Report for 1917–21, box 1, folder 7, MRC; J. P. Morris, letter to G. V. Newton, assistant commissioner of the Internal Revenue Service, March 10, 1920, box 1, folder 7, MRC; Doris Miller, interview by Fred Carpenter, October 6, 1975, tape recording, MRC. Doris Miller is the granddaughter of J. P. Morris and has lived in Coleman County all her life.

3. Doris Miller interview; Billie Marie Miller, interview by author, July 18, 1997, tape recording, MRC.

4. Morris family bible. The bible records the birth and death dates of the Morris and Miller families for five generations and is in the possession of Doris E. Miller of Shackelford County, Texas. The niece and namesake of Doris Miller cited in note 2 above, Doris E. Miller is the granddaughter of Mattie B. and lives on the Bluff Creek Ranch.

5. Doris Miller interview; Doris Miller, unpublished biography of J. P. Morris, no date, copy in the possession of the author; Morris family bible.

6. Doris Miller interview; Doris Miller, unpublished biography of J. P. Morris.

7. "Late J. P. Morris Founded and Directed Cattle Empire," *San Angelo Standard-Times*, February 6, 1938.

8. Ibid.

9. Jimmy Skaggs, *Prime Cut: Livestock Raising and Meatpacking in the United States, 1607–1983* (College Station: Texas A&M University Press, 1986), 130; Mattie B. Miller, Income Statement of the J. P. Morris Cattle Company for the Years 1921 and 1923, box 3 folder 2, MRC; Mattie B. Miller, Morris Cattle Company, Record Book 1921, 1922, and 1923, box 5, ledger 22, MRC.

10. Morris Cattle Company, Income Statement for the J. P. Morris Cattle Company for the Year 1924, box 2, ledger 22, MRC; Weather Bureau, *Climatological Data for the United States by Section, Summary* (Washington, DC: Government Printing Office, 1922–30), 97, 179.

11. Morris Cattle Company, Record Books, 1920–28, MRC.

12. Ibid.

13. Skaggs, *Prime Cut*, 130; Mattie B. Miller, Income Statement of the J. P. Morris Cattle Company for the Years 1921 and 1923; J. P. Miller Jr., interview

by author, July 16, 1997, tape recording, Southwest Collection, Texas Tech University, Lubbock, Texas (hereafter SWC). J. P. Miller Jr. is the grandson of Mattie B. and has spent most of his life in the ranching business in South Dakota and Texas. Well into the twentieth century it was common practice to wean calves off their mothers a day or two before they were shipped to market, which stressed the young calves a great deal. The stressed-out calves lost weight, became more prone to diseases, and often died during transport. After the trip to the buyers, which often took several days, the calves would often go off feed for days until they became accustomed to their new home and feed. Cattle raisers today wean their calves well before shipment, which allows the calves to get over the stress of weaning and get them used to eating grass or other feeds before going through the stress of being transported to a new environment.

14. John Buie, Worksheet for Individual Income Tax for 1918, box 5, ledger 11, MRC; J. J. Butts and F. D. Wright, attorneys-at-law, letter to Gilman & McMurray Attorneys, March 21, 1934, box 7, ledger 10, MRC: Morris, Buie, & Morris hired the law firm of Butts & Wright to help them with the legal problems surrounding Bluff Creek Ranch. The letter stated that Morris, Buie, & Morris purchased Bluff Creek on May 1, 1928. Payment of ten notes of $11,900 each for ten years, starting June 1, 1928 was stipulated. Morris, Buie, & Morris made only the first payment.

15. J. P. Morris, letter to Dr. E. L. Knox, November 5, 1932, MRC.

16. Morris Ranch, Income and Cost Statement of 1935, box 4, ledger 4, MRC; Morris Ranch, Account Book, 1909–1940, box 3, folder 5, MRC.

17. Mattie B. Miller, contract with her children, February 2, 1947, MRC.

18. J. P. Miller Jr. interview; Mattie B. Miller, contract with her children, MRC. Buerger's disease is a rare disease of the arteries and veins in the arms and legs. The disease causes inflammation and swelling of the affected limbs.

19. J. P. Morris, letter to his children, January 1, 1921, MRC; Mattie B. Morris Miller, contract with her children, MRC.

20. J. P. Miller Jr., interview by author, July 18, 1997, tape recording, SWC; Billie Marie Miller interview.

21. Mattie B. Miller, Ledger Book, April 1957–61, box 3, file 8, Morris Estate Collection, SWC.

22. Sam Ed Spence, "Rafter-3 Ranch, Herefords and History, *Cattleman*, August 1969, 45, 48.

23. Morris Ranch, Account Book, 1909–40, box 3, folder 5, MRC; Record of Cattle Sales, 1933–37, box 3, folder 5, MRC.

24. Morris Ranch, Ranch Account Book, 1909–49, box 3, folder 5, MRC.

25. Ranch Account Book, 1909–40; Record of Cattle Sales, 1933–37, box 3, folder 5, MRC.

26. Spence, "Rafter-3 Ranch," 45.

27. Spence, "Rafter-3 Ranch," 45, 48.

28. Morris Ranch, Account Book, 1909–40, box 3, folder 5, MRC.

29. Ibid.

30. Ibid.

31. Ibid.

32. Ibid.

33. Spence, "Rafter-3 Ranch," 48; Madge M. Graney, "She Taught Children to Love Books," *Christian Herald*, November 23, 1957, 96–101; Billie Marie Miller, interview by author, July 16, 1997, tape recording, Oral History Collection, SWC.

34. Graney, "She Taught Children to Love Books," 97; Billie Marie Miller interview, SWC.

35. Graney, "She Taught Children to Love Books," 97. A heifer is a young female cow that has not yet produced a calf. Once a heifer "dropped" a calf she entered the cow herd. A heifer will mature at about one year of age if she is managed well and has access to good grass and water. It is considered a good practice not to expose heifers to a bull until they reach at least six hundred pounds. The gestation period of a cow is similar to a human's, about nine months. Heifers are usually closely watched when it comes time for them to calf—they often need assistance for their first delivery. Sometimes a bull was purchased to breed to heifers, one that would "throw" a calf with a small birth weight.

36. Mattie B. Miller, Ledger Book, April 1957–61, box 3, file 8, MRC.

37. Doris Miller interview; Doris Miller, unpublished biography of J. P. Morris; Morris family bible.

Chapter 6

Mabel Doss, Mary Ketchum Meredith, and the Texas Fence-Cutting Wars

Brooke Wibracht

Historians portray the Texas Fence-Cutting Wars as a male-only civil conflict in which landless cattlemen and wealthy ranchers fought over natural resources. In this costly struggle that began around 1883 and lasted roughly until 1890, landless cattlemen disagreed with wealthy ranchers purchasing public land, alleging that the latter illegally enclosed grazing pastures and watering holes with barbed wire fences. Ranchers enforced their private property rights and did not allow others to use the natural resources, forcing landless cattlemen, who came to be known as fence cutters, into financial hardship. As tension between ranchers and cutters escalated into a statewide conflict, cutters retaliated by attacking the ranchers' barbed wire fences under the cover of darkness. They clipped the fences with wire cutters, pulled up posts, burned grass, and made death threats. In response, ranchers armed themselves and initiated patrols of their property lines. Once the ranchers and cutters used hostile tactics against each other, the Wars required government intervention.

In this rendering of the Wars, women's participation is altogether unrepresented. Women often inherited ranches when their husbands died and had to manage and retain property for their heirs. As this chapter will demonstrate, fence cutters targeted ranches regardless of whether a man or a woman owned the property. This forced women to fight for their rights as property owners. In contrast to male ranchers, female ranchers did not respond to the cutters with shotguns or threats. Instead they used diplomacy to stop the destruction of their properties.[1]

Rancher Mabel Doss was one woman who battled fence cutters and did so without using violent strategies. She employed two plans to stop them. Mabel relied on male associates to reach out to state officials on her behalf, and she tactfully confronted the cutters through published letters.

Mabel was born in Brunswick, Missouri, in 1854. She lived in Missouri until she attended Hocker Female College in Lexington, Kentucky, and she graduated with honors in 1872. Shortly after graduation she moved to Sherman, Texas, with her brother John Doss. Seven years later she married William Henry Day in January 1879. After their wedding, the couple moved to Day's twenty-two-thousand-acre ranch in Coleman County, Texas.[2] In 1879 Day used barbed wire to enclose pastures on his ranch and had plans to enclose the entire estate over time. Mabel spent her days beside her husband and observed his management of the land, cattle, and employees. After a little less than two years of marriage, the couple welcomed a daughter, Willie Mabel Day, on December 19, 1880. William Day died in June 1881 from injuries sustained two months earlier when he crushed his stomach on his saddle horn during a stampede.

Mabel assumed control of the estate when her husband died, and she learned that the ranch had accumulated more than $117,000 of debt. Her education and experience with her husband gave her the skills to handle the ranch's financial issues. After much consideration, she reached out to a friend from her college years in Kentucky who put her in contact with investors. She formed the Day Cattle Ranch Company, which was a two-hundred-thousand-dollar partnership comprising five Kentucky businessmen and her. The partnership represented a half-interest in her cattle for her investors, and Mabel retained full title to her land.[3]

Fence cutters initiated their attacks in Coleman County in the fall of 1883, and several ranchers, including Mabel, suffered property damage. Being the widow of a well-known cattleman, she had several

Figure 11. Mabel Doss Day Lea, circa 1883. Courtesy of Padgitt Ranch family collection.

influential and wealthy friends she could ask for help. The chief clerk of the Texas House of Representatives, John W. Booth, was one such friend. She wrote to Booth, outlined the issues she faced, asked him to talk with Governor John Ireland about the subject and inquired as to what he planned to do about fence cutting.[4] Her letter to Booth, however, did not generate any help for her ranch.

After her first letter failed to provide her any relief, Mabel changed tactics and decided to talk to the fence cutters. The only safe way for her to engage in a discussion was through the print media. She wrote a long letter that was published in the county newspaper, the *Coleman Voice*. She attacked the cutters' justifications for damaging private property. She argued that she owned or leased the lands that her husband enclosed, thus countering any claims of illegal fencing. Mabel highlighted the fact that she retained title or rights to the land, and that meant "no one has any right to grass or water except by my consent." Next Mabel maintained that she had placed, in accordance with the law, gates on the roads that led through her enclosed pastures. She did not complain of "parties tying down the wire so they could pass over any portion of my fence—only requested such parties to untie the wire so the stock could not pass out or in until my fence rider could get around to repair it." Lastly Mabel acknowledged that she had made an agreement with some out-of-state businessmen but contended that the business relationship would not bring financial harm to anyone. After addressing the cutters and their actions, Mabel spoke to her fellow ranchers, asking "Is there no recourse for us in the matter? Should you, as business and law-abiding men adopt any plan to protect your property I would beg to be considered as one among you."[5]

Mabel used her intelligence to force consideration of logical, reasonable arguments regarding the situation, never bringing up gender. She kept the focus on her rights as a landowner. By outlining how she not only followed the law but also tolerated damage to her private property, she demonstrated her desire to find a peaceful solution. From her perspective, using violence would not solve the problem. Mabel reasoned that since she did not break the law, the cutters should not attack her ranch. While she was correct in her assessment of her situation, her arguments did not address the cutters' grievances. They did not care that she followed the law; they only cared that Mabel's fences cut off their access to natural resources. Since Mabel made it clear that she would not remove her fences, the cutters were not motivated to listen to her appeals. In her letter, she did not plead and did not bargain with the cutters. Nor did she back away from the fight.

While Mabel avoided mention of gender, other county residents talked in the *Coleman Voice* about the cutters' violation of their gender roles. One man declared, "The Coleman County fence cutters might have had gallantry enough to have let Mrs. Day's wire fence alone. She may be rich, but she is a woman and that ought to go a long ways with true men." Another report stated, "The average fence cutter has very little respect for anybody or anything; and so far as gallantry is concerned he never heard of such a word. He who wantonly destroys the property of his neighbor, be he man or woman, is not a 'true man.'"[6]

Mabel's attempt at forcing a conversation with the fence cutters proved fruitless. They continuously cut her fences throughout the fall of 1883. Eventually she hired a line rider who patrolled her fences, but he did not stop the cutters. In just one instance a group of armed men with their faces blackened rode to Mabel's ranch during the day and brazenly cut ten miles of her fence, leaving a threatening note that promised more destruction and potential death if she repaired the fence.[7]

After this episode, Mabel wrote to Booth and asked for his help a second time. Booth telegrammed Adjutant General Wilburn H. King requesting that a company of Texas Rangers be sent to Coleman County to investigate the fence cutting.[8] Booth's telegram coincided with action taken by the governor in October 1883. The governor ordered Adjutant General King, along with a handful of Rangers, to Central Texas because fence cutting had become a statewide issue. In the fall of 1883, Texans sent hundreds of letters and telegrams to the governor's office asking for help, and the governor sent the Rangers to Central Texas where the most contentious fence cutting occurred. The governor's orders to send the Texas Rangers were not the result of Booth's telegram.

So that everyone could be heard and discuss the issue without bloodshed, the adjutant general and the Rangers spent a couple of days meeting with Coleman County residents. They listened to concerns of both ranchers and cutters. The *Dallas Weekly Herald* reported, "Adjutant-General King, in a conservative address, said that he had come to meet the people—to hear their grievances—so he could make an intelligent report to the governor of the true condition of the affairs."[9] Upon returning to Austin, King recorded his opinion on the fence cutting in Coleman County in the *Report of the Adjutant-General of the State of Texas* (1883). He said that he found the two warring groups to be upset with each other over the issues but that he did not find enough evidence to warrant arresting anyone. He added that he found "the most friendly feeling existed between many of the owners of pastures and those who openly opposed large pastures, and who thus gave encouragement to those who were lawlessly and secretly cutting down and destroying these enclosures." King stated that he believed those motivated to cut fences were limited to people who were feuding with other county residents. The adjutant general also reported that these situations were limited in number and that "the great body of the people in town and from the country were as good-natured, frank and friendly, and manifested as little sympathy with or encouragements of a bloodthirsty disposition on this all absorbing question as could be looked for in the most orderly community."[10]

Lastly he commented on the trustworthiness of the county authorities. He described the local constabulary as being sure of their abilities "to arrest any violator of the law that could be found," and he said that it was the opinion of the local government officials and citizens alike "that there was not the slightest danger of a resort to arms over this matter, in any organized form."[11]

Mabel had a different opinion than the adjutant general, and she expressed her disappointment in a letter to Booth. She wrote, "I suppose I ought to thank you for your efficient efforts in getting General King to Coleman. But I am sorry to know his going [to Coleman County] did not help me any. I have been informed that his going (that is the result of his being there) was worse than if he had not gone." She continued, "He had about ten Rangers with him. But that made no difference, since he refused to do anything."[12]

Recognizing that Booth, Coleman County authorities, and the state government would not stop the cutters from damaging her property, Mabel decided to stop asking for help from other people and published a second letter in the *Coleman Voice* to ask the fence cutters for mercy. She asked the cutters to consider that "I am not a man who can go with my cattle as they drift this winter, and hence as a woman I ask that you leave me at least my 'old' pasture." Mabel then outlined the reason for her actions in forming the business partnership with the investors. She stated, "Everyone knows that my husband's estate was greatly in debt,

and I was obliged to sell one half of the cattle for cash to pay this in-
debtedness off." Mabel tried to reassure the cutters: "Myself and little
child owns the land and one half of the cattle. These men will not come
here. I am to live here and run it myself. Thinking you may find it to
your pleasure and convenience to oblige me."[13]

The tone of this second published letter contrasts with that of the
first letter. Mabel employed her gender as a lens through which she
asked the cutters to view her and her financial situation. She repack-
aged her message to the cutters as a way to get them to stop attacking
her ranch, and she tried to use the privileges that her gender and her
status as a mother afforded her. In this letter she did plead, and she did
try to bargain. The cutters, nonetheless, did not allow her womanhood
to prevent them from accomplishing their goals.

The cutters continued to attack her fences. Mabel, however, was a
resilient woman who tried once again to stop the destruction of her
fences. She asked Coleman County real estate agents J. E. McCord and
E. A. Lindsay to write to Adjutant General King on her behalf. In their
letter to the adjutant general, they discussed the issues that she faced
and enclosed a list of people they thought were fence cutters. They
accused the cutters of being "small stockmen into communistic pro-
clivities" or greedy men who coveted her land and natural resources.[14]
McCord and Lindsay also requested that the adjutant general send an
undercover detective to the county to infiltrate the fence cutters' group
and report on their activities.

In King's response to McCord and Lindsay, he denied the land agents'
request for a detective, citing the expense of such an operation. He suggested that the "quiet but constant effort and watchfulness on this and of
the citizens instructed in connection with the presence and effort of the
Rangers in the infected district will accomplish more in suppressing this
villanry [sic] than can be obtained or secured by temporary work on the
part of even a superior detective."[15] However, King told McCord and
Lindsay that he would send Captain Samuel A. McMurray to Coleman
County to talk with Mabel and other ranchers, and he gave the captain
the authority to make decisions independent of the adjutant general if
he deemed it necessary. It is unknown whether the captain traveled to

Coleman County or talked with Mabel.[16] After this last letter to the adjutant general from male friends, Mabel halted her efforts to persuade others to help her defend her ranch.

Her efforts to protect her estate through diplomatic means did not produce results. Mabel's involvement in the Wars was long, unproductive, and quietly concluded when she stopped trying to get help. As the widow of a prominent cattleman, she enjoyed a place in high society. That social privilege, however, did not foster protection for her ranch. She corresponded with Booth, asking for his help and hoping his position in the state government could muster the governor to act and stop fence cutting. She also asked businessmen to write to the adjutant general and request the assistance of the state police. Simultaneously she engaged the cutters through the safety of a newspaper. Her first letter was direct and unapologetic and did not create a peaceful solution. Her second letter was polite and kind. Mabel tried to use her gender as a way to get the cutters to leave her ranch alone. She exhibited determination, and she demonstrated her intelligence by trying different ways to get her ranch out of the Wars.

She did not stop protecting her ranch; she simply decided to use one final tactic: patience. The state government sent the message that it was not going to help her or stop the cutters from attacking her property. It is possible that Mabel simply decided that it was more effective to wait out the unrest instead of repeatedly asking for help from a government body that demonstrated a lack of willingness to support ranchers in Coleman County. Other than sending the Rangers and the adjutant general to access the situation in Mabel's county, the state government did little.

Mabel not only managed her ranch through her husband's debts but also through the hardships of the Fence-Cutting Wars, withstanding the civil unrest and rebuilding her fences over time and on her own. In the end she defeated the fence cutters because she did not stop engaging in the cattle industry or conducting business, and she did not remain out of the public eye. Despite her financial debt, she was considered a wealthy rancher, and often newspapers ran stories on her business affairs, her travels, and social events she attended.

As an active member of the cattle industry, she attended conventions like the Range Association annual meetings. At the 1888 meeting in Denver, Colorado, her presence caused a stir. Several reporters found themselves eager to interview her or sit next to her at events. For example, one reporter commented:

> The original cattle queen of the West, Mrs. Mabel Day of Coleman . . . is really entitled to the roseate title, although she does not see why the ownership of a big bunch of cows should confer it on her. She is a lady of rare attainments, a thoroughly good business woman, and, being alone in the world, has learned how to care for herself. . . . She does not see why a woman should not be successful as a cattle owner, and scouts the idea of getting some one to help her. . . . She assures her admirers that she does not dash up and down the country after mavericks, in female road agent habiliments, with guns and knives galore all over her, but drives out as any other lady does.[17]

The reporter complemented her business skills as a cattle woman and noted that she successfully cared for herself without the help of a husband. Mabel's comments were enlightening. She emphasized that she retained her ladylike demeanor, and she downplayed the attention she received. As a female rancher, Mabel conducted herself so as to maintain her gender roles while participating in a male-dominated industry.

Another reporter found himself sitting next to Mabel at an event at the Range Association meeting, and he described her by saying, "Left alone to manage her deceased husband's business she has succeeded where men have failed. She is as self-reliant as a man and as womanly as a woman can be, the strong forces of her character being softened and subdued by the most delicate of feminine qualities."[18] In both articles, the reporters commented on Mabel's intelligence and business skills that she employed to succeed in the cattle business. Also, they reassured the readers that despite her involvement in the cattle business, she did not lose her womanly charm.

In addition to writing on her social engagements, newspapers speculated about her love life. A Colorado newspaper commented on her personal life by saying, "Mrs. Day refutes the story circulated regarding her adventure with a New York suitor who went to the Lone Star state to woo her, but it is believed to have some foundation in fact."[19] Not surprisingly, when she decided to remarry, her second marriage made the newspapers. The *Rocky Mountain News* printed: "Captain Joseph C. Lea of Lincoln county, New Mexico, with his bride, nee Mrs. Mabel Day, the cattle queen of Texas, is making a short visit to Denver. Captain Lea . . . is president of the Lea Cattle company and his union with Mrs. Day makes one of the strongest bovine combinations of the West, as well as a joining of chivalry and grace that is rarely equaled."[20] Mabel lived out her life on both ranches, often traveling between New Mexico and Texas to manage her business affairs in Coleman County. When she died in 1906, she passed her ranch, intact, to her daughter.[21]

While Mabel's efforts to stop the cutters were unsuccessful, another rancher, Mary Ketchum Meredith, had much more rewarding results. Mary, a Bexar County resident, also used diplomacy to deal with fence cutters. Mary corresponded with two Texas governors and asked for their help, which succeeded in getting the Texas Rangers to her ranch.

Mary Ketchum was born in Tennessee in 1834. She married John D. Meredith in 1858, and they had at least six children. In the early to mid-1870s she worked as the director of the Gaines Female Institute in Memphis, Tennessee. Sometime during the late 1870s, the family moved to Texas. Once the family moved, either her marriage fell apart or her husband died. The historical record is unclear as to her marital status. She referred to herself as a widow by 1880, but sources show her husband lived and worked in Corpus Christi. Despite the confusion surrounding her marriage, we know that she purchased land in Bexar County in 1883 and lived on the land with one of her sons.[22]

When fence cutters attacked her property in 1884, Mary traveled to Austin to meet with Governor Ireland. After days of waiting and not getting the chance to talk with him, she wrote a letter to get the governor's attention. She started, "I come to you in my sore trouble. I changed my home in San Antonio for a ranch 22 miles out from the city. I bought eight thousand acres & my young son has worked so hard to get it under fence." She then stated that they had just completed building twelve miles of fence, when that same week a "band of fence cutters" damaged five miles of it. She urged Ireland to act because "as fast as we run the wires the fence cutters will destroy them." She then remarked that her neighbors feared she would have her fences cut, but "we thought by putting gates at every pig trail they surely would spare us." This was not to be, however, as "in the five miles they cut there were three gates."[23]

After outlining the destruction of her fences, Mary then offered a solution to the problem. She wanted the governor to offer a reward to incentivize law-abiding citizens to report cutters. She also stressed the importance of the state government's assistance because she did not believe county authorities would help her. She wrote, "[They] wink at the whole affair and think all grass & farms ought to be open to the world." This, she believed, indicated that county authorities sided with fence cutters and would not fulfill their duties to investigate the crimes happening on her ranch. She concluded by letting the governor know she had been waiting for an audience with him but would wait one more day and "kiss your hand & be very grateful" if he would take the time to talk to her.[24]

It is unknown whether the governor met with her, but she did reap the reward of her efforts. Ireland forwarded her letter to Adjutant General King and directed him to send Rangers to look into the matter.[25] The adjutant general ordered two Rangers to investigate the case, which led to the arrest of one B. Dawson, charged with fence cutting.[26] Mary did not attend Dawson's trial, but she did not avoid seeing or talking with him. After his trial, he went to her ranch and confronted her, attested to his innocence, and claimed that he had been set up.[27]

Despite the Rangers' involvement in her case and the arrest of a fence cutter, the damage to her property did not stop; the fence cutters, however, did slow the frequency of their attacks. In 1887, just three years later, she was forced to once again ask for help. This time rather than travel to Austin to meet with the governor, she wrote to the new governor, Lawrence Sullivan Ross. In her letter she listed her previous encounters with the fence cutters and described her experience with the Rangers. She pleaded with Ross to help her and to send a "noble" ranger to her ranch to investigate and arrest the fence cutters. Mary professed that she had built her fences within the parameters of the laws and "made roads all thru the pasture. one road is 6 ½ miles long with a fence each side of it." She also explained why she thought the fence cutters kept attacking her property. Her land had previously been public land and was located along the Medina River; people in the area were accustomed to having access to the grass and the water. When she purchased and enclosed the land, she upset her neighbors who freely used the natural resources. Lastly, she told the governor that she had tried to deal with the cutters on her own by hiring a line rider. Her employee, however, was only one man and could not prevent the weekly attacks.[28] Ross referred the letter to the adjutant general, and the outcome of her second plea is unknown.

In her letters to Governors Ireland and Ross, Mary never mentioned that she was a woman. Instead she kept the focus on her rights as a landowner and all she had done to comply with the law. She built gates and asked county authorities to help her. She did not pick up a shotgun and conduct armed patrols of her property lines, as male ranchers had done, but had hired a line rider to protect her fences. These points made it imperative that the state government step in to help her. With the initial attack, which was during the height of the Wars, the state police lent its services and protected her ranch. The second attack was after the main period of unrest, which possibly explains why she did not receive the same level of protection from the Rangers. Despite the damage to her property, Mary fixed her fences and endured the unrest on her own.

After the Wars she involved herself in the growth of the surrounding communities by serving as the first postmaster for Macdona in Bexar County in 1887.[29] In addition to being a cattlewoman, she dabbled in the oil business and wrote to the *St. Louis Globe-Democrat* discussing her venture. She described her experience while digging two wells and asserted, "Won't it be fun if we find a million barrels of coal oil! We can pay all our neighbors for their starved and dead cattle and be rich ourselves, too. Good for Texas! If she can't grow rain she can heal our grief with floods of oil! Throw us a kiss, and wish us luck for dear old drough[t]-stricken Texas. Yours on a boom! Whoop la!"[30]

Mary earned a fine reputation and even in death remained well known in the area. In 1958 the *San Antonio Express and News* described her as "the founder of the town of Macdonna" and said she was known as the Queen of Medina. "Mrs. Meredith was often seen in the days of yesteryear riding in a carriage that is said to have once belonged to Gen. Grant."[31] She achieved her dream of making a life for herself and her son in the country. She lived on her ranch until she died in 1902.[32]

There are parallels between Mabel's and Mary's backgrounds and experiences during the Texas Fence-Cutting Wars. Both women had been born and raised in another state. Mabel moved to Texas with her family and later married a Texas cattleman while Mary married, had children, and then moved to Texas with her family. Her husband's death is recorded, as is her status as a widow; Mary's marital status is unclear although she claimed to be and acted as a widow. Mabel and Mary both conducted business without the supervision or assistance of a husband.

When their property and livelihood was threatened, both women acted with resolve. Mabel implemented two tactics to deal with the cutters. She urged male associates to use their positions in society to influence the governor and adjutant general, and she engaged fence cutters through published letters. Mary used one tactic. She directly requested help from two governors, once in person and once in a letter. The women engaged in the dialogue surrounding the Wars as men did, underscoring their status as landowners, not as women. They knew they had private property rights and did what they legally could as landowners to contend with the cutters. Both legally fenced in their pastures, built gates, hired line riders, and asked for help from county authorities. Unlike many of their male counterparts, they did not use violence to stop the destruction of their private property. With typical ranching tradition, both women withstood the civil unrest, rebuilt fences at their own expense, and passed their ranches to their descendants.

Mabel Day's and Mary Meredith's experiences overturn the assumption that the Texas Fence-Cutting Wars only involved men. The fractured nature of the historical record makes it difficult to know everything about the women's experiences. Nonetheless, their stories break the outdated mold of the Wars and open the scholarship for other historians to insert new perspectives. Interjecting women's histories and gender analysis to the Texas Fence-Cutting Wars modernizes the subject and produces a new thread in the scholarship that broadens historians' understanding of agrarian unrest in rural Texas.

Notes

1. Portions of this article are in the author's dissertation (forthcoming).

2. Coleman is the county seat of Coleman County in Central Texas; Sinclair Moreland, *The Texas Women's Hall of Fame* (Austin, Tex.: Biographical Press, 1917), 89–91; Elizabeth Maret, "Lea, Mabel Doss," *Handbook of Texas Online*, accessed October 6, 2015, http://www.tshaonline.org/handbook/online/articles/flejr; Eighth Census of the United States, 1860, Missouri, Schedule 1 (Free Inhabitants); James T. Padgitt, "Colonel William H. Day: Texas Ranchman," *Southwestern Historical Quarterly* 53, no 4 (1950): 347–66; William S. Speer and John H. Brown, eds., *Encyclopedia of the New West* (Marshall, Tex.: United States Biographical Publishing, 1881), 595–97; John Allen Peterson, "Day, William H.," *Handbook of Texas Online*, accessed October 6, 2015, http://www.tshaonline.org/handbook/online/articles/fda55; "The Day-Doss Nuptials at Sherman," *Denison (Tex.) Daily News*, January 28, 1879.

3. Padgitt, "Colonel William H. Day," 365–66, 358–59; "Personal," *Denison (Tex.) Daily News*, June 25, 1880; "Willie Mabel Day Padgitt," FindAGrave.com, accessed March 4, 2014, https://www.findagrave.com/memorial/33130076/willie-mabel-padgitt; "William H. Day," FindAGrave.com, accessed September 10, 2014, https://www.findagrave.com/memorial/64807692/william-h.-day; *Bourbon News* (Paris, Ky.), July 13, 1883; Maret, "Lea, Mabel Doss."

4. James T. Padgitt, "Mrs. Mabel Day and the Fence Cutters," *West Texas Historical Association Year Book* 26 (1950): 53.

5. Ibid., 57; *Austin (Tex.) Weekly Statesman*, October 11, 1883.

6. Padgitt, "Mrs. Mabel Day and the Fence Cutters," 57, 58.

7. Ibid., 59–60, 66.

8. Telegram from J. M. Booth to Adjutant General King, folder 4, box 401–5B, General Correspondence, Texas Adjutant General's Department, Archives and Information Services Division, Texas State Library and Archives Commission, Austin (hereafter ARIS-TSLAC).

9. "Fence Cutting: Both Sides on the Question Freely Discussed," *Dallas Weekly Herald*, November 1, 1883.

10. *Report of the Adjutant-General of the State of Texas* (Austin, Tex.: E. W. Swindells, 1883), 24.

11. Ibid.

12. Padgitt, "Mrs. Mabel Day and the Fence Cutters," 63.

13. Ibid., 65.

14. Letter from McCord and Lindsay to Adjutant General King, May 16, 1884, folder 14, box 401–4, Departmental Correspondence, Texas Adjutant General's Department, ARIS-TSLAC.

15. Letter from Adjutant General King to McCord and Lindsay, May 24, 1884, pp. 307–8, Letterpress 401–631, Departmental Correspondence, Texas Adjutant General's Department, ARIS-TSLAC.

16. Letter from Adjutant General King to Capt. Samuel A. McMurray, Capt. James T. Gillespie, Capt. Lamar P. Sieker, and Capt. George W. Baylor, February 4, 1884, pp. 99–102, Letterpress 401–631, Departmental Correspondence, Texas Adjutant General's Department, ARIS-TSLAC.

17. *Rocky Mountain News*, March 29, 1888.

18. *Rocky Mountain News*, March 28, 1888.

19. *Rocky Mountain News*, April 9, 1888.

20. *Rocky Mountain News*, June 30, 1889; "Wedding at Coleman," *Austin (Tex.) Weekly Statesman*, May 2, 1889.

21. "Lea, Mrs. Mabel Day," Case Number 2807, Dallas County, Texas, Probate Cases, 1846-Early 1900s, Dallas Genealogical Society, Portal to Texas History, http://texashistory.unt.edu/; "Funeral of Mrs. J. C. Lea," *Dallas Morning News*, April 6, 1906.

22. Lynda Lasswell Crist and Suzanne Scott Gibbs, et al., *The Papers of Jefferson Davis*, vol. 13, *1871–1879* (Baton Rouge: Louisiana State University Press, 2012), "Sources section," no pagination; "John Dabney Meredith," Corpus Christi Public Libraries, http://www.cclibraries.com/localhistory../oldbayview/index.php/list-of-burials/512-john-dabney-meredith; "Mary Ketchum Meredith," FindAGrave.com, accessed July 29, 2015, www.findagrave.com/memorial/36934597/mary-meredith; "Ketchum, Mary," Source Number 2583.020, Source Type Family Group Sheet, FGSE, listed as parents, U.S. and International Marriage Records, 1560–1900, Ancestry.com; Ninth Census of the United States, 1870, Shelby County, Tennessee, Schedule 1-Inhabitants; "Meredith, Mary K.," Bexar County and Atascosa County, Texas, "Texas, County Tax Rolls, 1846–1910," FamilySearch.org.

23. "Fence Cutting," *Atchison (Kans.) Daily Globe*, October 31, 1884; Letter from Mary K. Meredith to Governor Ireland, September 1884, folder 12, box 401–5, General Correspondence, Texas Adjutant General's Department, ARIS-TSLAC.

24. Letter from Mary K. Meredith to Governor Ireland, September 1884.

25. Ibid.

26. Scout Report, November and December 1884, folder 2, box 401–1182, Records of Scouts, Texas Adjutant General's Department, ARIS-TSLAC.

27. Letter from Mary K. Meredith to Governor Ross, February 5, 1887, folder 13, box 401–9, General Correspondence, Texas Adjutant General's Department, ARIS-TSLAC.

28. Ibid.

29. *Galveston Daily News*, February 14, 1887; Lula Lee McMeans, "Macdona, Texas," *Handbook of Texas Online*, http://www.tshaonline.org/handbook/online/articles/hwm01.

30. "A Boom for Texas," *St. Louis Globe-Democrat*, June 1, 1887.

31. "They Sew (When Not Chatting)," *San Antonio Express and News*, January 5, 1958.

32. She not only retained her Bexar County property but also purchased property in Atascosa County, Texas. Atascosa County is south of the city of San Antonio, and the county seat is Jourdanton. "Meredith, Mary K.," Bexar County and Atascosa County, Texas, "Texas, County Tax Rolls, 1846–1910," FamilySearch.org.

Chapter 7

Kathryn and Nancy Binford and the M-Bar Ranch

More than "Something in the Soil"

Renee M. Laegreid

In 1934 Kathryn (Kate) Cabot Binford's husband of twenty-four years died suddenly. Widowed, with two girls and a ten-thousand-acre ranching operation in the Texas Panhandle now in her hands, Kate faced daunting challenges, but there was no question whether or not to stay on the ranch. Relying on her own experience as a ranch wife, confident of help from hired hands and Barbara and Nancy, her teen-aged daughters, Kate remained on the ranch and oversaw its continued success. During the war years of the 1940s, Nancy joined Kate as a full-time partner, and the M-Bar Ranch would be a woman-owned and -operated family enterprise through Kate's death in 1987 and until Nancy's in 1998.

Women who operated ranches in frontier regions are often cast as exceptional. Whether exceptionally "good," like Kate Binford, resolutely continuing a ranch operation after the death of her husband, or exceptionally "bad," like the infamous Cattle Kate, women ranchers perhaps seem exceptional because history has recorded relatively few of their stories.[1] In the cases of those history has noted, awareness of the context in which they lived and the era-specific challenges they faced is essential to understanding their decision to take on the demands of ranch operations. That Kate Binford and later Nancy successfully managed and continued to develop the M-Bar is not a simple story of frontier feminism or cowgirl can-do attitudes derived from something in the Texas soil. The Binford story is rooted in place (the alignment of geographic location with ideas and values brought into the area by settlers), space (the varied social relationships that emerged in a particular place during a certain time), and gender relationships formed in a specific place and space.[2]

Place forms the core of the Binford's story, bringing together environmental characteristics of the Texas Panhandle with social, economic, and cultural ideas introduced into the region by midwesterners during the late 1870s. The sense of place in the northwestern corner of Texas differs from other parts of the state. As historian Terry G. Jordan assessed, "The state of Texas is really a series of regions, each one with a unique cultural history and expression."[3] Prior to Anglo intrusion, the land that became the Panhandle region of Texas had a history of its own, one that would shape and be shaped by the circumstances of its midwestern immigrants.

On a map today, the Texas Panhandle juts north from the main part of the state. New Mexico defines its western border, and Oklahoma forms its northern and eastern boundaries. The physical characteristics of the land, though, pay no attention to these lines. The Panhandle is part of the southern reaches of the Great Plains—flat, arid, and treeless.[4] These high plains, tilting almost imperceptibly from an elevation of about four thousand feet at the northwestern border to about one thousand feet at the southeastern edge of the Panhandle, receive more rainfall than many other parts of the state, about eighteen to twenty-one inches per year.[5] For millennia, bison and other wildlife thrived on the lush grasslands, while the Canadian River and its tributaries provided water and winter shelter for animals and Native peoples who called the region home.

Unlike in South Texas, Spanish explorations that began with Coronado in 1541 did not result in settlement or occupation, leaving the area free from European influence.[6] In the 1820s, after Mexico won independence from Spain, the newly formed government warily allowed US ranchers and cotton growers into the southeastern part of Texas—Mexico's northern frontier region—to populate it and protect it from the threat of foreign takeover. The movement of cattle ranchers followed a path along the Southeastern Pine Barrens Belt, which, according to Jordan, "provid[ed] a major natural route for the westward expansion of the Carolina cattle culture" through Georgia, Florida, Alabama, Mississippi, and Louisiana, and into southeastern Texas.[7] Even after the Mexican-American War, when Texas became part of the Union, gold seekers traversing the Panhandle did not stop to settle. "In the early to mid-nineteenth century," M. Scott Sosebee notes, "pioneers viewed West Texas and its grasslands with curious wonder or sometimes an obstacle to cross on the way to great fortune elsewhere."[8] Fear of Comanche and Apache attacks also encouraged travelers to hurry across the region. Therefore, while the southern and eastern portions of Texas continued to increase in population, the Panhandle remained relatively free from Anglo intrusion.

By the mid-1800s, though, changes were underway. Sosebee writes, "Three things—the displacement of Indians, extermination of bison, and development of cattle trails to northern markets—created favorable conditions for extending ranching into West Texas."[9] European diseases had significantly reduced the population of Native peoples, and the US government's mission to confine Native peoples to reservations, executed by the US Army, "weakened the Comanche hold on lands they had long dominated in West Texas."[10] While the Civil War slowed the process of Anglo intrusion into Texas, after the war the federal government stepped up its efforts to remove the remaining Native peoples to reservations, which they did with the combined efforts of the US Army and bison hunters, who decimated the animals Native Americans depended upon for survival. Removal of Native peoples after the Red River War of 1874 cleared the way for Anglos to move into the region during the late 1870s, when the state of Texas began selling its public lands. As Sosebee notes, "Enterprising cattlemen bought range land on which they grazed their animals, or leased pastures to other stockmen," inaugurating the western range cattle industry.[11]

The timing of Anglo movement into northernmost Texas is critical to understanding the Panhandle's sense of place—the dovetailing of location and imported values and ideas—in the region Kate Cabot would call home. Land speculators and settlers entering the Panhandle brought with them a far different worldview than the Anglos who had transferred plantation-style agriculture to the southern part of Texas half a century earlier. Midwesterners who had benefited from a post–Civil War industrial economy spearheaded land acquisition in the Panhandle. Regarding Vega, H. Allen Anderson writes:

> As early as 1879 the area was opened by the state for homesteading. N. J. Whitfield became the first settler in the fall of 1899 when he purchased the future townsite. Early in 1903 he sold a 100-foot southern strip across the county's southern end to the Choctaw, Oklahoma, and Texas (later the Rock Island) Railroad as a right-of-way. In May of that year A. M. Miller and Howard Trigg surveyed the townsite. . . . In 1907 ranchers Pat and John Landergin purchased part of the LS Ranch from the Swift Company. Working in association with the Pool Land Company of Amarillo, they brought in more prospective settlers for the community.[12]

These settlers brought with them, as the following deed indicates, particular attitudes toward the land:

> The State of Texas known all now by Theses Grayson County Presents: What we Jof. Gunter and W. B. Munson of the County of Grayson in the State of Texas for and in consideration of the sum of one dollar and the further consideration of the delivery to us of one thousand style (2) two half (1/2) case Wheeler and Wilson sewing machines by A. B. Howard of St. Louis Mo. the receipt of which is hereby acknowledged have this day sold and do by these presents grant bargain sell and convey unto A. B. Howard of the City of St. Louis and the State of Missouri the following described track of land situated in the Counties of Oldham and Deaf Smith and State of Texas.[13]

These Missouri businessmen, Gunter and Munson, considered land purchases in the Panhandle as an investment, and they considered land itself to be like any other commodity to be sold or traded for money—or sewing machines—according to their commercial strategies. A distinct sense of place, then, developed early on as Anglos invested and moved into the Panhandle, firmly connecting the region with midwestern views of commercially oriented ranching and farming, along with midwestern progressive ideals.

At twenty years of age, Kathryn "Kate" Cabot moved with her family to a ranch in Oldham County that was five miles outside the growing town of Vega. She later recalled, "My parents, Will and Ethel Cabot, moved to Oldham County, Texas in 1908, because of my mother's health. My [older] brother, Norman, and my [younger] sister, Ferne, and I moved to Texas with them."[14] The Cabots had likely been drawn to the area by land speculators in Amarillo advertising newly available tracts of land to midwesterners.[15] The push of having to find a less humid climate for Mrs. Cabot and the pull from opportunities offered by speculators encouraged the Cabots to leave their hometown of Prophetstown, Illinois, where they had been successful farmers since the 1830s.[16] They had raised corn, oats, barley, and potatoes on their Illinois farm, and they had operated a breeding stable specializing in Percheron and Standardbred horses. The Cabots planned to restart their stock growing and agriculture business on the Panhandle's high plains.[17]

Unlike Texas settlers a generation earlier, the Cabots traveled to their new home site by rail instead of horse and wagon, taking the Rock Island train from Illinois to the end of the line: Wilderado, Texas. In 1908 the Panhandle was still a frontier region, and Kate later remembered, "The train stop[ed] twice from Amarillo to Wilderado to cross gates. Some kids waited for the train, opened and closed the gates behind it and had for it the privilege of a free train ride back to town."[18] As the line to Vega would not be complete until the following year, the Cabot family unloaded their goods from the train in Wilderado, a bustling young town of one hundred residents, and continued by wagon for roughly fifteen miles to their ranch, five miles southwest of Vega.[19]

In 1907, the year before Kate and her family arrived on their new ranch, Eugene Binford had traveled to Oldham County to check the land his father, Thaddeus Binford, had recently purchased.[20] "In 1908, I met Gene Binford," Kate recalled. Binford was again visiting land owned by his father.[21] No descriptions of how they met exist, although in small frontier towns like Vega and Wilderado, news of the arrival of an attractive young woman must have circulated quickly among the eligible men in the region. Gene was certainly eligible. An 1896 graduate from the University of Michigan law school, Gene returned to his hometown of Marshalltown, Iowa, to practice law. Described by his family as an athletic man who enjoyed sports and the outdoors, Gene must have found the vast, open spaces of Oldham County and its possibilities a better fit for him than practicing in an urban law office. Kate recalled, "He never really wanted to be a lawyer, so he talked his family into letting him live on the ranch."[22] Perhaps meeting Kate factored into his decision.

After a two-year courtship, Kate and Gene married on August 2, 1910, among friends and family on the Arcadia Ranch in Oldham County and "started their lives together ranching six miles west of Arcadia."[23] Gene had begun investing in land prior to their marriage, and for the first year or so they lived in an old trapper's cabin on land he had bought with a banker from Amarillo.[24] In either 1911 or 1912 they moved to Gene's father's ten-thousand-acre ranch, the present site of the M-Bar Ranch.[25] Carmen Goldthwaite writes that the Binford property, located northwest of Wilderado, spread "south of the Canadian River and north and west of Palo Duro Canyon. The region, with its lush grasses and the Canadian River winding through, so recently home to vast herds of bison, was well suited to raising cattle and crops."[26]

Kate and Gene brought to their marriage not only a shared love of horses and the outdoors but also a middle-class progressive worldview. Progressivism in the United States was "a many-sided reform movement that emerged in the final years of the nineteenth century, flourished from about 1900 to 1920, and faded away by the early 1920s." The impetus for reforms arose from rapid social and economic changes after the Civil War, reflecting "a growing, if temporary, consensus among Americans that major changes in the late nineteenth-century had produced unwelcome, un-American imbalances in their society."[27] Reformers sought to solve diverse social problems brought about by these rapid changes, fortuitously creating new opportunities for middle-class women outside the confines of the Victorian-era domestic sphere. Women advocated for access to education, professional careers, and full legal enfranchisement, all the while challenging traditional conceptions of what women could accomplish. Gene's sister, Jessie Florence Binford, exemplifies the educated, socially conscious women of the era;

she created a career for herself in Jane Addams's famous Hull House settlement home in Chicago.[28] Kate's mother, Ethel Cabot, embraced new opportunities for women, taking up photography and developing and mounting her own photos.[29] Kate too had been encouraged from youth to take on activities, like breaking and training her own horses, that pushed the traditional gender boundaries. The Progressive idea of allowing women more active roles in society, to determine their own lives beyond the confines of a domestic sphere, provided a common base of understanding for Kate and Gene.

The couple's relationship also reflected Progressive ideas to reform the Victorian concept of marriage. "Among the middle class," writes Christina Simmons, "the economic, spiritual, and reproductive meaning of marriage" was the target of reformers who, since the early 1900s, had seen the need to give "a new meaning to marriage for new times," one that would encourage egalitarian relationships based on mutual affection, respect, and shared interests.[30] While the term "companionate marriage" did not emerge until the mid-1920s, a decade after their wedding, Kate and Gene benefited from these new attitudes. Living on a large ranch, in an era in which midwestern Progressive values encouraged women to move beyond a strictly defined sphere, Kate and Gene could look forward to working together as a shared adventure without controversy.[31]

And there was plenty of work to do. Their first home, the two-room trapper's cabin, did not have running water. Close by there were "some springs across a little draw for water supply. Later they dug a well by hand, put a windmill over it and piped water to the house." They traveled by horse and buggy to Tulia, Texas, about eighty miles away, to buy their first herd of purebred horned Hereford cattle, camping out along the way. An oft-repeated story about Kate is that, "as they were finishing cutting their choice out of the seller's herd, he [the seller] asked Mr. Binford teasingly to let his wife choose the bulls. She did, too, and as she was thru with her pick the man just sighed: she ruined me! Mrs. Binford had gotten the best of his bulls." The seller learned too late that despite her feminine appearance, Kate had developed a keen eye for recognizing quality breeding stock, a skill she would be admired for throughout her long life.[32]

After driving their new herd to their ranch, Kate and Gene began improving their property, introducing many firsts into the region. In an autobiographical essay for Oldham County's centennial celebration, Nancy Binford wrote, "In the 1920's, my father tried new land conservation methods of control and confined cattle feeding."[33] The M-Bar did not have many fences when Kate and Gene moved onto the ranch, and so they could design their pastures to rotate cattle. A local newspaper reported, "Husband and wife, with a team and a wagon full of post and wire, went around building fences in their free time from attending the stock . . . and farming a few acres."[34] Aware of the need to supplant grazing with hay—perhaps inspired by stories of the Great Cattle Die-off of 1886–87, only twenty years prior to Binford's land purchase—Kate and Gene raised all of the hay for their cattle's needs.[35]

The M-Bar also became one of the first ranches in the region to take part in the US Remount Service, a federal program designed to increase the supply and quality of horses for military needs. Beginning in 1908 the government supplied top-quality stallions from eastern breeding farms to civilian ranchers; the government usually bought back male colts for military use, allowing the breeder to keep fillies as future brood mares to improve their herd quality.[36] Joining in the program would have been a natural for Kate, having grown up on a horse-breeding farm and, according to a local source, having always "admired and owned blooded horses."[37] Using government-supplied thoroughbreds to sell to the US Cavalry proved an excellent low-cost business strategy for improving their own stock. Together they built up the ranch, with Kate working and riding "side-by-side with her husband . . . [and] when Gene traveled, she managed alone," doing the ranch work, domestic work, and managing the remount stallions.[38]

A newspaper reported, "Mrs. Binford . . . said she practically lived on [a horse] before her children were born."[39] Still, Kate's activities building the ranch did not relieve her of domestic chores. Progressive gender reforms did not include radical changes to women's responsibilities around the home or ranch. According to newspaper accounts, Kate "chopped wood, hauled water, washed on a wash-board, tended the family garden and turned the stakeout into a home."[40] And she bore children. In 1912 Kate drove herself to town in a wagon, Gene accompanying her on horseback, to await the birth of their first child (their son, Thaddeus Cabot Binford, died a week after being born). Pregnant again in 1914 and anticipating another journey to town, Kate wrote, "Next fall we will be in our Ford when we go. I have decided to have Gene and I get one together and I will learn to runn [*sic*] it first and then Gene afterwards."[41] Their second son did not survive his first day. In 1918 Kate had her first daughter, Barbara. Nancy was born in 1921.

Kate and Gene's interests and activities extended beyond the day-to-day work of ranch life. Typical of Progressive-minded, middle-class couples, they dedicated themselves to building their community and serving social causes. Kate became a well-respected figure in Wilderado for her work with children and the County Welfare Board. She served as president of the PTA in the Wilderado elementary school Gene helped organize. Kate also was involved in local business, as a board director of a producers' grain cooperative from the organization's beginning.[42] And both Kate and Gene were active in Wilderado's First United Methodist Church.[43] Gene's background in law involved him with their community too. He joined a special branch of the Texas Rangers, the Loyalty Rangers, authorized by the Hobby Loyalty Act of 1918 to "combat threats of subversion and disloyalty" inspired by the Mexican Revolution and World War II, and served from June 1918 to February 1919.[44] Kate and Gene also combined work and play. Prior to Vega becoming the county seat in 1915, Kate recalled, "I remember so well the trips to old Tascosa, when Gene had to serve on the jury. We would drive over in our democrat [a horse-drawn buggy]. We were usually there for a week and camped out at the Turner place, where we visited and fished."[45]

Frontier conditions notwithstanding, place and space in the early-twentieth-century Texas Panhandle allowed for gender relations to evolve differently there than in the southern and eastern parts of the state. In her study of frontier women who settled southeastern Texas as it opened during Mexican control (during the decades after the 1830s), Anne Patton Malone describes the difficulty elite and middle-class, or yeoman, women had as they adjusted to raw frontier conditions. Malone notes that wives of yeoman farmers, craftsmen, and tradesmen, while versed in Victorian gender mores, fared better than elite women, since they had more experience working alongside their husbands and could–adjust to physical work outside the home, knowing that their efforts would hasten their return to the domestic sphere.[46] Fifty years after the period Malone describes, Kate enjoyed her experiences building the ranch alongside her husband without considering her situation as backsliding. The shift in gender expectations that had occurred over the fifty years between southeastern Texas settlement and Panhandle settlement diminished the imperative for women to go back into the domestic sphere when their economic conditions improved.

Kate and Gene lived on and worked the land owned by his parents, doing so for nearly twenty years. Their businesslike approach to the ranch, combined with progressive, information-based land management and stock-raising, helped create a successful operation. When Gene's mother died in 1929, the land became theirs.[47] Having title to the ranch became a financial boon during the tough Depression years. While oil had been discovered in the Panhandle in 1921, Gene did not begin leasing gas and oil rights on the ranch until 1930.[48] The lease money helped. The Binfords began plans to build a thirteen-room Spanish pueblo type of house, "considerably different" from the rough ranch house they had shared for so long."[49] When Nancy was born in 1921, the ranch house still lacked indoor plumbing.

Farming and ranching during the Depression and drought was tough business. Living in Oldham County, right in the geographic center of the Dust Bowl, meant struggling with high temperatures, lack of rain, and dust: dust storms, dust accumulating like snow drifts across fields, and illnesses related to the omnipresent dust, for humans and livestock alike.[50] Everyone struggled to keep crops and cattle alive. A local newspaper reported: "During the 'dirty thirties' Mrs. Binford said it was necessary to grub out bear grass and grind it as a cattle feed." Kate recalled, "By feeding them bear grass ensilage we had the biggest and finest cattle we ever had on the place."[51] This must have been a sad irony for the Binfords, to have such high-quality cattle but the lowest market prices for cattle that ranchers had seen in a long time.

Beginning in the summer of 1934, a series of tragedies hit the close-knit Cabot/Binford family. Kate's mother, chronically ill for many years, died on July 20, and not five weeks later her father died.[52] Then, as Kate recalled, "in October of the same year, Gene passed away," succumbing to pancreatic cancer at the age of sixty-two.[53] Despite the loss of her husband, the decision to stay on the ranch would not have been a difficult one for Kate. The M-Bar had been her home for nearly twenty-five years, and she had been a partner in its operation since the first days of her marriage. In "Kathryn Binford, A Pioneer Woman," the anonymous author writes that "at the time it was something unheard of, for a woman to handle a ranch their size alone."[54] Yet her decision to stay was likely based on the fact that she was *not* alone. Kate had the support of her siblings—brother Norm and sister Ferne—who both lived nearby with their families, from her neighbors, from her teen-aged daughters, and from members of the community in which both Kate and Gene had been actively involved since their arrivals in the Panhandle.

Kate assumed responsibility for the ranch during the Great Depression, an era when women across the West found themselves shouldering new responsibilities as husbands, sons, fathers and brothers moved away to find work. To keep the ranch going, Kate worked long and hard hours. She would recall "feeding stock with wagons in the snow, farming with a team and rudimentary implements and later on with tractors, and handling the thoroughbred remount stallions stationed on the ranch."[55] Yet she did not face these challenges alone. "Everybody helped her over the hard years with their advice and on branding and round-up days neighbors like Jay Taylor's ranch on the West and LS (Ware Ranch) North were there making it easier."[56] During harvest she could count on hiring good help, "and the families who worked for her were like her own family and some stayed for many years, and they still help as neighbors on spring and fall round-ups or in any need."[57] And she had her daughters, Barbara, fifteen, and thirteen-year-old Nancy.

With Gene gone, Kate became mother, father, and friend to the girls, deepening an already strong bond and connection to the ranch. From infancy, the girls had accompanied their parents as they worked around the ranch, sleeping in a carriage as Kate did chores near the house, bundled up in the back of a wagon while Kate and Gene fed cattle, and later learning the day-to-day operations from them. Now with Kate directing their activities, the Binford women worked together as a team. Nancy would later recall coming home from school and finding at their bus stop their horses that Kate had saddled and left for her and Barbara, along with a list of chores to complete as they rode the two and a half miles to the ranch house. Sometimes Kate used somewhat unconventional methods to take care of cattle. Nancy's most terrifying experience, she would remember, was trying to rope sick calves from the car while Kate drove. "She was a terrible driver!"[58] But they got the work done.

The sense of shared responsibility that developed among the Binford women did not change the expectation that both Barbara and Nancy would go to college. Barbara attended Texas Technical College (now Texas Tech University) in Lubbock, returning home during her college years as she could to help on the ranch. She met and married W. H. Hayes, an air force officer during World War II; after the war, the couple moved to Colorado Springs, Colorado.[59] Barbara embraced the cultural trends that enveloped the post–World War II United States, which encouraged couples to seek normalcy in marriage and family. Nancy took a different path. She attended Texas Tech, graduated with a degree in physical education in 1943, taught physical education for one year at Lubbock High School, and then returned to the M-Bar in the spring of 1944. "During the war," Nancy recalled, "my mother needed help here on the ranch."[60] Within a few years, mother and daughter formed a joint partnership in the ranch, each contributing their experiences, talents, and ideas for improvement. In a statement that captures her parents' progressive attitudes, Nancy remarked, "If you don't grow, you go backwards, [and] the only thing worse than making a mistake is making a mistake and not profiting by it."[61] With two generations of combined education and experience, Kate and Nancy kept the ranch successful.

If 1930s gender trends that Kate, Gene, and other settlers brought to the Panhandle contributed to Kate's ability to run the ranch, evolving gender ideas in the region helped shape Nancy's decision to return to the ranch and become a partner. In an interview, Kate later told reporters, "We never thought about it, about just women running it

Figure 12. Nancy Binford with her quarter horse mare, Blondie B., at the Tri-State All Girls Rodeo. Courtesy of National Cowgirl Museum and Hall of Fame, Fort Worth, Texas.

[the ranch]. You just do what needs to be done."[62] Yet the combination of location and culture that developed in the late 1870s, and the social relationships that emerged from that sense of place, contributed to the ease in which Kate could continue the ranch and Nancy return to it and enjoy her lifestyle as an educated, middle-class ranch woman without disrupting gender norms. In fact, when seen in the context of her cohorts, Nancy exemplified those norms. Her friends from throughout the Panhandle, most born in the 1920s, reared on ranches, and most with at least some college education, all participated in their family's daily ranching operations.

Nancy's friends, second-generation ranch women like herself, had been reared to be competent in what people outside the region might have considered encroaching on the masculine sphere. Within the Panhandle, however, the skills and accomplishments of these ranch daughters were not considered mannish or unfeminine. Anne Patton

Figure 13. Nancy Binford (*left*) and her friend Thena Mae Farr in a photo to publicize the first all-female rodeo. Courtesy of National Cowgirl Museum and Hall of Fame, Fort Worth, Texas.

Malone argues that the frontier experience masculinized women, yet a certain symmetry developed between masculine activities to contribute to the family economy and the continuing expectation of feminine behaviors.[63] The gender dynamics in this particular place and space allowed women to own their own cattle herds, work alongside brothers and fathers, and take on responsibilities and pursue opportunities and hobbies that outside the region might be considered proto-feminist ("Nancy welds and works with metal . . . she made fireplace fixtures, curtain hangers, bathroom racks and lighting fixtures") yet remain squarely within the gender norms for the Texas Panhandle.[64]

During Nancy's high school years, female ranch friends competed with and against one another in local "sponsor contests," combinations of beauty pageant and equestrianism, an example of the easy mixture of feminine and practical demands. Nancy won her first sponsor contest at age fifteen, and in her senior year of high school she won the title of

"Sweetheart of the Amarillo Riders." Her good friend Thena Mae Farr also garnered numerous titles in beauty contests and sponsor contests.[65] In 1947 the two became partners in organizing the Tri-State All Girl Rodeo, the first rodeo organized by women for women participants.[66] The rodeo proved such an enormous success that Binford and Farr decided to continue the partnership organizing "all-girl" rodeos. Newspaper accounts described the women contestants as doing everything in the arena that men did but always looking fashionable and "acting like ladies." During the late 1940s and into the early 1950s Nancy had owned and operated a western wear store in Amarillo, perhaps contributing to her and her friends' sartorial elegance.[67]

The tight bonds between Nancy and her friends, beginning with their days competing at sponsor contests, at ranch rodeos, would continue throughout their lives. And the women certainly knew the ropes. Ruby Gobbles, daughter of a ranching family and close friend to Nancy, often stayed at the Binford ranch to help with summer responsibilities. She later recalled that Kate worked the girls so hard that she and Nancy looked forward to a weekend of rodeo just to rest.[68] Dude Barton recalled the miserable yet necessary chore of "doc'ing calves for screw worms," which always seemed to come at the hottest, muggiest, time of the year.[69] Likewise, Jackie Worthington, Thena Mae Farr, and the other all-girl rodeo competitors participated in every aspect of their families' ranching operations. There was no aspect of ranch work these women did not know, and, like cowboys who gather to help during roundups, these friends came together to help on each other's ranches when needed.[70]

Nancy and Thena disbanded their rodeo production partnership in 1953, and Nancy devoted more of her time to refining her cattle herds, breeding and training quarter horses for cutting horse competitions and, later, horse racing. The *Amarillo Globe-Times* noted, "She has owned racing horses off and on through the years but it wasn't until three years ago that she registered her racing colors, turquoise and white with a black chaparral, and decided to go into the racing business and out of the show business."[71] The remount breeding program, which her parents had embraced during the early years of their marriage, helped to create a new breed of western horse: the American

Quarter Horse. Nancy worked with local horse breeders in Amarillo, helping organize the American Quarter Horse Association and the National Cutting Horse Association. She was reported to be among the first quarter horse owners to ever exhibit cutting horses outside the Southwest when she exhibited a horse in Chicago in 1948.[72]

In the late 1950s, Nancy phased out her racing stable. Kate was getting older and needed more help with the day-to-day operations with the cattle. When Kate moved off the ranch into an assisted-living facility in town in the 1980s, Nancy continued to confer with her mother about ranching. "She is still my partner and knows more about the ranch than I ever will," she admitted. After Kate's death in 1987, Nancy hired a female manager and horse trainer from Spain, Daniela Bernabeu, to help her with the demands of the ranch's cattle and haying operations.[73] At her death in 1998, Nancy willed the ranch to Bernabeu, continuing the Binford tradition of the M-Bar as a woman-owned and -operated ranch in the Texas Panhandle.[74]

It is challenging to find and trace women who, like Kate Binford, chose to remain on a ranch after a husband's death. Like so much of women's history, finding their stories involves peaking around the edges of extant evidence, sifting through shards of their histories—in a letter, on a note in a family bible or the back of a faded photo, or a serendipitous mention in an old newspaper clipping. But it is a challenge worth pursuing. Despite the paucity of documents, understanding Kathryn and Nancy Binford's success as women ranchers can be understood by connecting a specific place, the Texas Panhandle, with the Progressive, midwestern, and upper-middle-class values settlers brought with them that created a unique space. The gender dynamics within that space allowed both mother and daughter to embrace opportunities outside of traditional domestic responsibilities without upsetting local gender norms. Knowing the larger context of their lives broadens our understanding of the diversity of experience among western women and, importantly, often provides a corrective to stereotypical assumptions of women in Texas and throughout the West.

Notes

1. Lori Van Pelt, "Cattle Kate: Homesteader or Cattle Thief," in Glenda Riley and Richard W. Etulain, eds. *Wild Women of the Old West* (Golden, Colo.: Fulcrum, 2003), 154–76.

2. Theoretical construct derived from Doreen Massey, *Place, Space, and Gender* (Minneapolis: University of Minnesota Press, 1994).

3. Terry G. Jordan, *Trails to Texas: Southern Roots of Western Cattle Ranching* (Lincoln: University of Nebraska Press, 1981), 44.

4. Walter Prescott Webb, *The Great Plains* (Boston: Ginn, 1931), 3–9.

5. Frederick W. Rathjen, *The Texas Panhandle Frontier* (Lubbock: Texas Tech University Press, 1998), 2, 11.

6. Ibid., 38.

7. Jordan, *Trails to Texas*, 44.

8. M. Scott Sosebee, "Agriculture, Ranching, and Rural Life," in *West Texas: A History of the Giant Side of the State*, Paul H. Carlson and Bruce A. Glasrud, eds., (Norman: University of Oklahoma State, 2014), 196–210.

9. Sosebee, "Agriculture, Ranching, and Rural Life," 199.

10. Ibid., 197.

11. Ibid., 199.

12. H. Allen Anderson, "Vega, TX," *Handbook of Texas Online*, accessed June 23, 2016, https://tshaonline.org/handbook/online/articles/hlv07.

13. Land Deed book F-1, p. 36, County Clerk's Office, Oldham County, Texas.

14. Kathryn Binford, "Kathryn Cabot Binford," *Oldham County Book, 1881–1981*, 2. Kathryn Binford Files, National Cowgirl Museum and Hall of Fame, Fort Worth (hereafter NCM).

15. Anderson, "Vega, TX."

16. "Charles Willis 'Will' Cabot," FindAGrave, accessed June 22, 2016, https://www.findagrave.com/memorial/85617271.

17. Kathryn Cabot Binford Scrapbook, Kathryn Binford Files, NCM.

18. "Kathryn Binford: A Pioneer Woman," Kathryn Binford Files, NCM.

19. Anderson, "Vega, TX." The Cabots later moved twenty-two miles east to a ranch near Bushland, Texas, closer to the growing city of Amarillo.

20. "Honored on Birthday," *Vega (Tex.) Enterprise*, December 5, 1963, Kathryn Binford Files, NCM.

21. Nancy Binford, "Nancy Binford," *Oldham County Book, 1881–1981*, 2, Kathryn Binford Files, NCM.

22. Kathryn Cabot Binford Scrapbook.

23. "Honored on Birthday."

24. Terry Hiller, "An Indisputable Texas Elite," *Sunday (Fort Worth) Star-Telegram*, January 24, 1982.

25. Sources differ on when they moved to the Binford ranch. "Katherine Binford: A Pioneer Woman" states they moved in 1911; newspaper accounts indicate 1912. Katherine Cabot Binford File, NCM.

26. Carmen Goldthwaite, *Texas Ranch Women: Three Generations of Mettle and Moxie* (Charleston, S.C., History Press, 2014), 161.

27. Walter Nugent, *Progressivism: A Very Short Introduction* (Oxford: Oxford University Press, 2010), 1, 2.

28. "Jessie Binford," newspaper clipping, n.d., Nancy Binford File, NCM. In its entirety: "Jessie Binford of Hull House is among five Americans cited by the Volunteers of America for bringing the Christmas spirit to the nation all year round. Others are Gen. Wainwright, Brig. Gen. Huldah Smith, authoress Louis Baker [*sic*], Cleveland Indians manager Lou Boudreau and radio's Ralph Edwards."

29. Kathryn Cabot Binford Scrapbook.

30. Christina Simmons, *Making Marriage Modern: Women's Sexuality from the Progressive Era to World War II* (Oxford: Oxford University Press, 2009), 107; Jean V. Matthews, *The Rise of the New Woman: The Women's Movement in America, 1875–1930* (Chicago: Ivan R. Dee, 2003), 96–98.

31. It was "a region of mainly white Anglo-Saxon Protestants." Rathjen, *Texas Panhandle Frontier*, 37.

32. "Kathryn Binford: A Pioneer Woman."

33. Nancy Binford, "Nancy Binford," 2.

34. "Kathryn Binford: A Pioneer Woman."

35. Kathryn Binford, "Katheryn Cabot Binford," *Oldham County Book*, 2.

36. Phil Livingston and Ed Roberts, *War Horse: Mounting the Cavalry with America's Finest Horses* (1905; repr., Albany, Tex.: Bright Sky Press, 2003).

37. "Honored on Birthday."

38. Hiller, "Indisputable Texas Elite."

39. "Chaparral Emphasizes Turf Polish," Kathryn Binford Files, NCM.

40. Hiller, "Indisputable Texas Elite."

41. From back of postcard. Kathryn Cabot Binford Scrapbook.

42. "Honored on Birthday."

43. "Kathryn Cabot Binford," *Amarillo Daily News*, October 2, 1987, Kathryn Binford Files, NCM.

44. Charles H. Harris III, Frances E. Harris, and Louis R. Sadler, *Texas Ranger Biographies: Those Who Served, 1910–1921* (Albuquerque: University of New Mexico Press, 2009), xv, 33; "Loyalty Rangers," Genealogy Trails History Group, http://genealogytrails.com/tex/texasrangers/loyaltyrangers.html.

45. Kathryn Binford, "Kathryn Cabot Binford," 2.

46. Anne Patton Malone, *Women on the Texas Frontier: A Cross-Cultural Perspective* (El Paso: Texas Western Press, 1983), 21–22.

47. Gene's father, Thaddeus Binford (1839–1917), bequeathed the ranch to his wife, Angelica Beasley Binford (1844–1929). "Eugene Beasley 'Gene' Binford," FindAGrave, accessed June 22, 2016, https://www.findagrave.com/memorial/37750391.

48. Oldham County, Texas, Reverse Index to Deeds, Deeds of Trust, Etc., A–D, from May 31, 1878–1992, 1930. Oil and gas leases in the names of Barbara, Nancy, Gene, and Gene's unmarried sister, Jessie.

49. "Chaparral Emphasizes Turf Polish."

50. Richard White, *"It's Your Misfortune and None of My Own": A New History of the American West* (Norman: University of Oklahoma Press, 1991), 478.

51. "Chaparral Emphasizes Turf Polish."

52. Ethel B. Cabot, Texas, Death Certificates, 1903–1982 Images Archives, accessed June 22, 2016, http://www.archives.com/; "Charles Willis 'Will' Cabot," FindAGrave, accessed June 22, 2016, https://www.findagrave.com/memorial/85617271.

53. Kathryn Binford, "Kathryn Cabot Binford"; Eugene Beasley Binford, Texas, Death Certificates, Fold3.com, accessed June 22, 2016, http://www.fold3.com/image/85057867. Thanks to longtime friend Michael Miller for deciphering the cause of death on Gene Binford's death certificate.

54. "Kathryn Binford: A Pioneer Woman."

55. Kathryn Cabot Binford Scrapbook.

56. "Kathryn Binford: A Pioneer Woman."

57. Ibid.

58. Goldthwaite, *Texas Ranch Women*, 164.

59. Kathryn Binford, "Kathryn Cabot Binford," 2.

60. Quotation from nomination form, Nancy Binford File, NCM.

61. Betty Linn Noll, "Area Ranch Woman Has Capable Hand on Rein," clipping, November 20, 1962, Nancy Binford File, NCM.

62. Hiller, "Indisputable Texas Elite."

63. Malone, *Women on the Texas Frontier*, 22.

64. Noll, "Area Ranch Woman Has Capable Hand on Rein."

65. Renee Laegreid, "A New Kind of Community Rodeo Queen: Sponsor Girls at the Texas Cowboy Reunion," in *Riding Pretty: Rodeo Royalty in the American West* (Lincoln: University of Nebraska Press, 2006), 71–94, 188.

66. Renee Laegreid, "'Performers Prove Beauty and Rodeo Can Be Mixed': The Return of the Cowgirl Queen," *Montana: The Magazine of Western History* 54, no. 1 (Spring 2004): 53.

67. "Area Horsewoman Nancy Binford Dies," *Amarillo Globe-Times*, July 29, 1998.

68. Ruby Gobble, interview by author, October 26, 2006.

69. Mary Ellen "Dude" Barton, interview by author, Matador, Texas, March 15, 2008.

70. Ray Davis, "Jackie Worthington and Her Cowgirl Crew," *Western Horseman*, March 1975, 54, 55, 138, 139.

71. "Area Horsewoman Nancy Binford Dies," *Amarillo Globe-Times*, July 29, 1998.

72. "No Man's Land: NQHA Show in Chicago," Nancy Binford File, NCM.

73. "Nancy Binford, Binford Ranch, Wilderado," *Texas Highways*, July 1986, 41.

74. Nancy did not marry and therefore did not have family to inherit the M-Bar ranch. Her sister's family had no interest in taking over the ranch. For transfer of the M-Bar to Daniela Bernabeu, see Oldham County, Texas, Land Records, Grantee Index 10-30-1992 to 12-31-1999, p. 29.

Chapter 8

Alice Gertrudis King Kleberg East
Loving the Land

Cecilia Gutierrez Venable

Alice Gertrudis King Kleberg East (1893–1997) descended from a long line of women who loved their environs. These women guided, shaped, and educated themselves to become active business partners and stewards of the land. Alice's grandmother Henrietta Chamberlain King reported that her father instilled in her the idea to be the "master of her own destiny . . . [and] that a girl didn't have to be a clinging vine."[1] Henrietta King learned Spanish and later taught children in South Texas. After marrying Richard King she moved into a crude jacal on Santa Gertrudis Creek and performed tasks she deemed important, including educating children and ministering to the sick. The Kineños (as Mexicans working on the King Ranch were known) called her La Madama. Henrietta expanded her ranch holdings, fostered the development of her land, and designated certain parcels for schools, churches, and hospitals. She loved the ranch and made sure she instilled that attribute in her five children. One of Henrietta's three daughters, Alice Gertrudis King Kleberg (1862–1944), especially loved the ranch. When Henrietta King was in St. Louis with her daughter also named Henrietta, Alice assumed the duties of the household, cared for her father, and helped him with his business. Alice King also continued her mother's practice of working with the vaqueros. She would raise her children on the ranch and teach them to love the land.[2]

Consequently, it is not surprising that her daughter Alice Gertrudis King Kleberg East carried this heritage to her children.

Alice East acquired land and worked alongside her spouse (Tom Timmons East Sr.) and children to improve their stock and expand their landholding. She aided her vaquero families monetarily and helped them educate their children, and they called her La Madama, just as they used the title of endearment for her grandmother. She lived an interesting life, but little has been written about her, partly because she shied away from attention and found her enjoyment working the land she loved.

Figure 14. Alice Gertrudis King Kleberg East. Courtesy of East Foundation Archives.

The lack of historical attention to these and other ranching women is not unusual. Although women's labor contributed to ranch growth and profit, they rarely received payment, and this lack of compensation or proof of their work allowed the marginalization of women by scholars of agricultural and range activities. In any case, measuring women's undertakings through payment proves difficult since women often held temporary positions in this sector because of male-favored land inheritance. Men acquired property, and women coped with changing heads of household, with different expectations of how they should contribute to the ranch. Women who rode, branded, and roped cattle on the range could suddenly be expected to work only in the home. Others found themselves pushed to marry for financial support or had to seek employment in town. Since some women did not spend their lives working the ranch, they appear in history, if at all, as intermittent players, their talents marginalized.[3]

In South Texas, however, this was not always the case. Because of the adoption of Spanish land practices, women inherited land and often controlled ranches. The spouses of these women acknowledged their wives' independent ownership, as in the case of Ciprian Hinojosa, who stated, "My wife [is the owner of her brand] and interests, which exist in her property." He made known that she did not make decisions for his stock and property and more importantly acknowledged that he did not have an interest in her holdings. This conception of women owning and running their property and stock was typical to the region, and this phenomenon was reaffirmed by pioneers of South Texas's painted horse desert who found women owning and branding animals with their brands, not their spouses'.[4]

It is not surprising that women who operated small ranches escape historical notice, but one would think that those who commanded larger parcels of land should have garnered some attention. For the most part that does not seem to be the case. For example, several books document the activities of the King Ranch, but few concentrate on Henrietta King's influence. When the young bride was left alone on the ranch during the Civil War, while her husband attended other businesses, she ran the ranch. After the war she maintained the business because Richard King traveled extensively due to his other interests.

At the time of Richard's death, she controlled her holdings, and King Ranch historian Tom Lea remarked, "It has become a kind of legend in round numbers, that King left his widow half a million acres along with half a million dollars debt."[5] Henrietta amassed more than 1,175,000 acres with 94,000 cattle by the time of her death.[6] Most accounts of this era attribute the growth of the ranch to Alice East's father, Robert Kleberg. While Kleberg had his mother-in-law Henrietta King's consent to operate the ranch, she still made important decisions about the business after her husband's death. Her daughter Alice aided her mother with operations, just as she had helped her father before his death. Despite this, both women remained at the historical periphery until Lisa Neely's *King Ranch and Kingsville* (2011), followed by Jane Monday and Fran Vick's *Letters to Alice* (2012). Both works discuss some of Henrietta King's and Alice Gertrudis King Kleberg's contributions to the ranch. These books, however, end their study with Alice Gertrudis King Kleberg East as a child, so the continuation of Henrietta and her daughter's legacy still await study.[7]

––––––

Alice Gertrudis King Kleberg was born on January 9, 1893, in Corpus Christi. She was delivered by a family friend and renowned physician, Arthur Edward Spohn, who had also delivered her brother Richard Mifflin Kleberg in 1887 and her sister Henrietta Rosa in 1889, and would later deliver Robert J. Kleberg Jr. in 1896 and Sarah Spohn Kleberg in 1898. When the newborn Alice could safely travel, the family returned to the Santa Gertrudis ranch and the King home, which accommodated their growing family and visitors.[8] The Klebergs moved to the King home after Richard King's death in 1885. Their cohabitation at the Santa Gertrudis allowed the elder Alice Kleberg to care for her mother and Robert Kleberg to help in the running of the ranch. The Kleberg children in the meantime learned to ride at a very young age and arose early in the morning to mount their horses and run the range. Young Alice loved to ride, and she spent most of her days in the saddle. She enjoyed the outdoors and the solitude.[9] Alice also learned to hunt and joined her father, friends, and family in this activity. She learned to rattle deer horns in the hopes of attracting a buck and to use a dog to flush out quail. The land supported a wide range of animals, and the family hunted a variety of birds, deer, and javelina. Their catch provided food for the family and the vaqueros. Alice became an accomplished hunter and would hone her skill as an adult.[10] Her husband decades later wrote in his journal, "Mrs. East did not have so much luck [because] she killed about five," indicating that he was used to his wife bringing home more food than that.[11]

As the Kleberg children matured and entered school, the family moved to Corpus Christi. Henrietta King, along with Alice and Robert Kleberg, designed a house located on upper Broadway overlooking the bluff with a view over the bay. The twenty-room mansion became the family's home during the school term. Robert practiced law in town and enmeshed himself with the city's politics. However, governing the ranch forced him to spend more time away from the family, and at the end of the school year the family excitedly left town for the ranch.[12]

When young Alice Kleberg reached her teens, her mother and grandmother decided that she and her sister Henrietta should attend a prominent eastern school to complete their education. The elders chose Belmont College in Nashville, located on seventy-five acres of Joseph and Adelicia Acklen's Belle Monte estate. The school opened its doors in 1890 to provide elementary to junior college education for girls and young women. Alice attended Belmont in 1910 at the age of seventeen. While at this institution she acquired the title "Girl of the Golden West," and, unlike her sister Henrietta, was active in athletics, serving also as treasurer of the Tennis Club. She had a love for physical activity and the outdoors. Both girls joined the riding club, which favored English-style saddles instead of the western saddle Alice preferred.[13]

In 1911 Alice moved to Gunston Hall for Young Ladies in Washington, DC, run by Civil War veteran Beverley R. Mason. The institution had a wonderful athletic department, and Alice continued to play tennis while adding another sport, basketball. She flourished at this institution and became the captain of the basketball team as well as a member of the Dramatic Club and Theta Chi sorority. She continued her studies of German and literature and also studied French.

While Alice was active at the school, her classmates described her as being "rather hard to know." Her friends also noted that she loved the ranching life. Their sentiment reflected Alice Kleberg's independent spirit and her need for solitude. Although Gunston Hall provided a distinguished education, it lacked the comforts of her South Texas home, its smells, early-morning dove calls, deer moving through the brush, and poikilotherms slithering to catch the warmth of the sun, which Alice missed.[14]

The Wild Horse Desert had captured Alice's heart with its natural beauty, but the state was in economic chaos at this time. Many farmers and ranchers worked on another person's land from sunrise till the end of the day. The number of tenant farmers and sharecroppers in Texas climbed to two hundred thousand in 1910, and this form of labor continued stifling the dreams of many who wanted to own their own land. Along Texas's southern border, the Mexican Revolution brought refugees escaping their country's violence, revolutionaries searching for support, and lawless individuals seeking to benefit from the bedlam created by fear, discontent, and violence. These events left many Texans anxious about their future and position.[15]

At the Santa Gertrudis ranch, the anxiety was manifested through a disgruntled worker who set the King home ablaze in January 1912. Alice, home on winter break from school, was in her room asleep when the house caught fire. As the family assembled outside, they noticed she was missing. Her uncle Al Kleberg rushed back into the house, found Alice asleep and oblivious to the fire, and carried her to safety where she joined the family and watched as flames engulfed their home. Alice ran to the bell tower and rang the bell to awaken the ranching staff, but there was little they could do. They all gathered with the family and watched the flames lick the walls until only ashes remained.[16]

Henrietta King wanted her home rebuilt, and, while construction began, Alice returned to school in Washington and later graduated from Gunston Hall in 1912. After the ceremonies she returned to the ranch where she could ride and work with the vaqueros.[17] Alice rode her horse and worked all day, as hard as any of the employees. Although she liked school, she was glad to be back at the ranch.

Alice loved ranching and the land, so it was not surprising when she fell in love with twenty-six-year-old Tom Timmons East.[18] The lanky East had a stellar reputation as a businessman and cowboy by the time he and Alice started dating. East hailed from sturdy stock: a great grandfather had fought with Andrew Jackson in the War of 1812; a grandfather had helped establish the thriving city of Kaskaskia, Illinois; and his father, Edward, had fought with the Tenth Illinois Cavalry Regiment during the Civil War. When Edward made Texas his home, he first owned a ranch in Archer County and for several years purchased stock from L. T. Clark of Tom Green County. Eventually he moved to Kingsville and ranched there till his death.[19] Tom and his brothers formed a company called East Brothers and, among other interests, operated the San Antonio Viejo Ranch in the South Texas brush country that included the Nueces and Rio Grande basins near present-day Hebbronville. Alice and Tom had much in common—they both loved the land and the ranching life—and after a short courtship

Figure 15. Alice Gertrudis King East (right) and daughter Alice (Hattie) East (left). Courtesy of East Foundation Archives.

they married at 8:30 a.m., January 30, 1915, in the music room of the Santa Gertrudis ranch house. Her sister Henrietta was the maid of honor, and Caesar Kleberg was best man. Minerva King played the piano while Dick Kleberg sang "Till the Sands of the Desert Grow Cold." At the conclusion of the wedding, the bride and groom traveled to the San Antonio Viejo Ranch for the night and awoke early the next day to ride into Agua Dulce to buy some young heifers with their wedding money.[20]

The couple worked their ranch in the South Texas brush country, roping, branding and laboring alongside their vaqueros. They lived frugally, reinvesting their earnings to improve their land and stock and protect their holdings in a troubled Texas economy. Many Texans along the border continued to be affected by the Mexican Revolution. Mexicans living on the border also felt stressed. They watched their supplies dwindle and were forced to support the army and revolutionaries in the area. Consequently many turned to banditry themselves to survive.

Pancho Villa, the popular Mexican revolutionary general, wreaked havoc up and down the border, and on March 9, 1916, he crossed into New Mexico to pillage the town of Columbus, killing eighteen US citizens. The Thirteenth Cavalry sprang into action and killed one hundred of the insurrectionists and inflicted numerous injuries on others, forcing them to retreat. When President Woodrow Wilson learned about these events, he sent Major General John J. Pershing to capture Villa, but Villa continued to evade his pursuers. The border violence finally spilled onto the San Antonio Viejo Ranch.[21] On March 17, 1916, when Alice and Tom returned home, Tom walked to the barn, opened the door, and saw forty armed Mexicans. Alice, unaware of what awaited her, drove around the back and was soon surrounded by the bandits. Tom ran back to the workers' camp for help and sent word to the Rangers in Hebbronville. The next morning the thieves loaded the ranch's food supplies, rounded up some horses, and rode off. Tom arrived with the Rangers, and they tracked the bandits for twenty-five miles before catching them. They killed one of the marauders and injured several others as they fled across the border, leaving their spoils behind.[22]

The Easts continued to enrich their holdings, although Alice limited her activities for a short time because of the birth of their first child, Thomas Timmons East Jr., on January 2, 1917. When both mother and baby were strong enough, she returned to the saddle.[23] Alice's grandson Mike East later remarked that his grandmother recalled that she would feed and change his father and then suspend him from a tree so that she could work cattle.[24] The baby would be shaded by the tree and be protected from animals.

The year Tom Jr. was born, South Texas experienced a harsh drought. Lack of rain in the region has periodically plagued the cattle business. In 1864 Thomas J. Noakes, an English resident in South Texas wrote in his diary:

> The country is dried up; the cattle and horses are starving for want of water, the river being too salty for them to drink. . . . The country is most desolate, the high wind blew the dust and sand, which covers everything in clouds filling the atmosphere, and confining the range of vision to a small space. . . . [I see] the distressed and starved look of the cattle, the thousands (may safely say) of dead and dying which land at the mouth of the river or lay about on the shore together with the dried and look of the country for there is not a green thing to be seen, and I rode to one watering place on this side where the place was entirely blocked up with bogged cattle, there being twenty-seven in one bunch, first a row was bogged next to the shore, and then another row which had climbed over them to [drink], and that way they were bogged three and four feet deep. You could stand at one place and count a hundred and twenty, some dead and some alive.[25]

Noakes posited that the lack of rain in South Texas had forced the cattle to the Nueces River in search of water, but there they found the salinity too high for them to drink. Without the rain to flush the river into the Gulf, the water had stagnated, and the starving animals caught in the quagmire of the muddy bank, and too weakened by lack of food and water to extricate themselves, died in their tracks. In 1917 the cattle on the San Antonio Viejo Ranch fortunately had some water from wells and springs to drink. However, they lacked vegetation due to the drought. Tom burned needles off the cactus to feed the cattle to stave off starvation. Other ranchers who could not buy feed hauled their stock to market, and the influx caused cattle prices to plummet. While drought conditions pressured the industry, US involvement in World War I also affected it, because some ranch hands joined the war effort. These severe conditions eventually drove the Easts to mortgage their ranch to Alice's grandmother, Henrietta King. While the Easts no longer held titles to their place, Alice and Tom could remain in their home, working for the King Ranch.[26]

While it was probably hard for the Easts to give up control of their ranch, they continued to raise and improve stock and watched their family grow. Son Robert Claude was born in 1919, followed by Alice (Lica) Hattie in 1920.[27] These additions required Alice to relinquish some of her activities around the ranch, but with the aid of *vaqueras* who helped with the children, she was able to continue working. In 1925 the East family received the devastating news that Alice's grandmother, Henrietta King, had died.[28]

Alice and Tom continued to be very frugal and work the San Antonio Viejo Ranch. They taught their children to ride horses almost as soon as they learned to walk, and when their labor was needed, they missed school.[29] The couple worked as partners and must have had disagreements but found common ground, Tom hints in his journal:

Today is my 13th wedding anniversary, and I can truthfully say there has been lots of ups and downs in [the] past 13 years. [I] have fought lots of battles . . . have not lost any yet—but several come out as a draw.[30]

The next decade brought grief to the family once again when Tom, visiting his mother-in-law at the Santa Gertrudis ranch, suffered a stroke and died on November 29, 1943. His passing devastated family and friends, and the family received condolences from politicians, ranchers, executives, and members of the military. Ralph E. Ireland ("Irish"), one of Tom's best friends, stationed in India at the time, wrote to Alice, "What a wonderfully pleasant memory he has left with Elizabeth, the boys and myself. . . . Tom and one [other] retired army officer were the only two men I've known since the last war that I'd whole heartedly trust. . . . [He was] far deeper and more sincere than most. It hurts too much to write any more now."[31] Tom was buried in Chamberlain Burial Park near his parents but his remains were later moved and re-interred next to his family.[32]

The running of the ranch now fell to Alice East, her children, and the vaqueros. Alice was close to her workers. She cared for them, helped some with their visas, and helped others to become citizens. Alice and other members of her family drove the children of the cowboys to school and took them to see a doctor. Alice also provided the workers time off, so they could visit their families across the border. The East family continued to work alongside their employees, although at times Alice micromanaged their activities. Rogerio Garza, a ranch hand, re-marked that after Alice, Robert, Lica and the vaqueros worked cattle and loaded them on the trailer, Alice would recount the stock to make sure the tally was correct. She was meticulous in handling the animals and with the business.

In 1951 Alice negotiated with the King Ranch to acquire the San Antonio Viejo Ranch in exchange for her 20 percent interest in the King Ranch, left to her in Henrietta's will. With this transaction she now had her home back, and each member in her family contributed to the continued success of her holdings. Her eldest son, Tom Jr., excelled as a businessman and worker, but in 1984 suffered a fatal heart attack.[33]

Alice's two other children, Robert and Lica, remained at the San Antonio Viejo Ranch throughout their lives. Alice had clearly passed the love of the land to her children. While Alice still rode horses until she was eighty, her children oversaw ranch operations, relying heavily on Alice's counsel.

As Alice, Tom, and Lica aged, they discussed the disposition of the land after they were gone, and they decided to form a foundation. Lica died in 1993, and four years later Alice died at the age of a 104, out-living two of her children and all of her siblings. The surviving son, Robert Claude, finalized the future of the ranch by forming a nonprofit known as the East Wildlife Foundation (now the East Foundation). This foundation consisted of the land the family had accumulated, which comprised six different ranches totaling more than two hundred thousand acres. The foundation carried on the family's heritage of securing the land for livestock and wildlife in perpetuity. In accordance with its goals and mission, the foundation opened the ranch for educational and research purposes, which promoted ranching while protecting the land and its ecological balance.[34]

Several scientific endeavors, including weather monitoring and grass studies, took place on the ranch. Birds and their migration, nesting, and habitats were monitored, as were carnivores, which included the endangered ocelot. The white-tailed deer on the ranch, a significant draw for hunters in South Texas, garnered genetic studies and monitoring of their food source and its effects. Nilgai antelope roamed the ranch, and their interactions with the native white-tailed deer were studied.

In October 2014 the ranch opened its gates to local fifth graders in the Rio Grande Valley. Arriving by bus, they spent the day learning about the flora and fauna of the area. Many of these children had never witnessed wildlife in their natural habitat or the workings of a cattle ranch. From February 9 through February 12, 2016, the ranch held another outing for children. A group of nine hundred eighth and ninth graders from Zapata, Bruni, Hebbronville, Falfurrias and San Isidro participated in several workshops, including ones about careers in natural resource management, hunting laws, game management, and technology. The children's unique experience on the ranch is part of the legacy of Alice East's love of the land and the ranching life.[35]

Alice East's life represents those of other women in South Texas who have worked on ranches and loved the land. Few of these women are well known because they sought anonymity and commanded little attention. They were not the antithesis of the genteel women of their time, just individuals who honed their skills and expertise to forge a living on the land. These women not only cared for their homes but also enjoyed the outdoors, the saddle, and the freedom of working on the range. A perfect example of the versatility they possessed can be found in a little brown journal that Alice kept. There she wrote down instructions for knitting a baby cap and a recipe for Grape Nuts pudding and "melts in your mouth" muffins along with instructions on how to set the pump in the well house. This journal reveals the well-rounded life Alice East led. She was as comfortable in the kitchen as she was on the land.[36]

Alice Gertrudis King Kleberg East was schooled in the fineries in life. She had attended boarding schools and received etiquette lessons but did not limit her existence to the women's sphere of home and family, guardianship of morals, and comfort for her husband. Instead she proved herself to be an able partner. Like her grandmother and mother before her, she ran the business, and it prospered under her care. Alice East continued the tradition of loving the land and passed this on to her children. Not only did she foster their ability to live off the land, she also taught them how to do so. While her husband was active in teaching the children how to rope and ride, Alice also helped them develop their skills on the range. In fact, her daughter, Lica, competed against her in barrel racing, and Lica won. Children in Lica's era often learned these skills from their fathers, brothers, or other males, but Alice East and women like her changed that.

Alice operated in two worlds, the traditional women's sphere and the male-dominated ranching world. She gained respect in both and lived a full life. It is fitting that the ranch that evoked such passion and happiness for Alice and the East family is now a foundation that promotes research and education. Alice East's legacy of loving the land will be passed on for generations through the children and researchers the foundation inspires.

Notes

I would like to thank Neal Wilkins with the East Foundation for reading a draft of this work. His insight regarding the East family history is exceptional, and I appreciate his input.

1. Carmen Goldthwaite, *Texas Dames: Sassy and Savvy Women throughout Lone Star History* (Charleston, S.C.: History Press, 2012), 45.

2. Jane Clements Monday and Frances Brannen Vick, *Petra's Legacy: The South Texas Ranching Empire of Petra Vela and Mifflin Kenedy* (College Station: Texas A&M University Press, 2007), 301.

3. Elizabeth Maret, *Women of the Range: Women's Roles in the Texas Beef Cattle Industry* (College Station: Texas A&M University Press, 1993), 15.

4. Teresa Jordan, *Cowgirls: Women of the American West* (Lincoln: University of

Nebraska Press, 1982), xiv; Armando C. Alonzo, *Tejano Legacy: Rancheros and Settlers in South Texas, 1734–1900* (Albuquerque: University of New Mexico Press), 240.

5. Tom Lea, *The King Ranch* (Boston: Little, Brown, 1957), 139, 264, 271, 471.

6. Jay Nixon, *Stewards of a Vision: A History of the King Ranch* (Kingsville, Tex., 1986), 22.

7. Lisa A. Neely, *King Ranch and Kingsville: A Match Made in South Texas* (Kingsville: King Ranch and Grunwald Printing, 2011); Jane Clements Monday and Frances Brannen Vick eds., *Letters to Alice: Birth of the Kleberg-King Ranch Dynasty* (College Station: Texas A&M University Press, 2012).

8. Monday and Vick, *Letters to Alice*, 136–37; Tom Lea, *King Ranch*, 508.

9. Delayed birth certificate of Alice Kleberg, East Foundation archives, San Antonio (hereafter EF); Monday and Vick, *Letters to Alice*, 139; Lea, *King Ranch*, 561–62.

10. Neely, *King Ranch and Kingsville*, 335; photographs in EF.

11. Notebook written by Tom East, EF.

12. Monday and Vick, *Letters to Alice*, 140–41.

13. *Bachelor Girl* (Gunston Hall yearbook), 1910, 1912.

14. Ibid., 1912.

15. Randolph B. Campbell, *Gone to Texas: A History of the Lone Star State* (New York: University of Oxford Press, 2003), 347–49.

16. Monday and Vick, *Letters to Alice*, 144–45; Lea, *King Ranch*, 570.

17. *Bachelor Girl*, 1912.

18. Monday and Vick, *Letters to Alice*, 56, 123; Lea, *King Ranch*, 573.

19. J. Evetts Haley, "Jim East Trail Hand and Cowboy," *Panhandle-Plains Historical Review* 4 (1931); Marvin Hunter, ed. *The Trail Drivers of Texas* (Austin: University of Texas Press, 1924), 564.

20. Lea, *King Ranch*, 573. This was a very popular romantic song for its day and appropriate for a wedding. The refrain: "Till the sands of the desert grow cold, / And their infinite numbers are told, / God gave thee to me, / And mine thou shalt be, / Forever to have and to hold." George Graff Jr. and Ernest R. Ball, "Till the Sands of the Desert Grow Cold" (1911), *Historic Sheet Music Collection* 1107, Digital Commons at Connecticut College, http://digitalcommons.conn-coll.edu/sheetmusic/1107.

21. Michael C. Meyer, "Felix Sommerfeld and the Columbus Raid of 1916," *Arizona and the West* 25, no. 3 (Autumn 1983), 213–14.

22. Lea, *King Ranch*, 588–89.

23. *Texas Birth Index, 1903–1997*, Texas Department of State Health Services.

24. Author's personal communication with Mike East in 2015 at EF.

25. Thomas John Noakes, *Diary of My Life Commencing Janr'y 10, 1858*, vol. 2, 1863–1864, Corpus Christi Public Library.

26. Terrence Henry, "A History of Drought and Extreme Weather," *State Impact*, November 29, 2011, https://stateimpact.npr.org/texas/2011/11/29/a-his

tory-of-drought-and-extreme-weather-in-texas. A *Galveston Tribune* report on July 24, 1925 ("Drought Hurts Texas Cotton") noted that the continued lack of rain caused the cotton seed not to germinate, leaving a very small cotton crop. The article also noted that the number of hay bales had dropped dramatically.

27. *Texas Birth Index, 1903–1997.*

28. Neely, *King Ranch and Kingsville,* 27.

29. Ibid.

30. Tom East Journal, EF.

31. Letter from Ireland to Alice East, December 28, 1943, EF.

32. Scrapbooks in EF.

33. Bruce Cheesemen, "Alice East Celebrates 100th Birthday," newspaper clipping, EF; documents, applications, and letters from workers, EF; oral history interview with Rogerio Garza by Neal Wilkins, EF.

34. East Wildlife Foundation Newsletters in EF.

35. Ibid.

36. Alice East Journal, EF.

Chapter 9

Frances Rosenthal Kallison

Historian at Home in the Saddle

Hollace Ava Weiner

Frances Rosenthal Kallison began life as a city girl, learning dressage on the dray horses that pulled carts to and from her family's Fort Worth furniture store. She never dreamed that someday she'd be a western-riding aficionado, performing with a blue-ribbon posse, naming newborn calves at a South Texas ranch, or qualifying for the National Cowgirl Hall of Fame. As comfortable with a lead rope as with a fountain pen, she registered bulls, kept breed books up to date, and wrote articles documenting mid-twentieth-century ranch life—from the travels of an itinerant blacksmith to the precision steps of the Bexar County Sheriff's Mounted Posse Auxiliary, of which she was a charter rider.[1] Her Victorian upbringing and northern college credentials served as a counterpoint to the relaxed western traditions of the family she married into. Cognizant of the lure and lore of the cowboy, during World War II she opened the family ranch to busloads of GIs, serving barbecue and encouraging soldiers to saddle up for a ride on the range. "They had heard about the Wild West, and they were eager to see . . . a real Texas working ranch," she would say.[2] Frances's fabled hospitality, along with her imperious manner, crisp writing style, and exacting scholarship landed her a seat on the Bexar County Historical Commission. There, during two decades of involvement, she received the honorific "Hidalgo de San Antonio de Bejar," an aristocratic Spanish title reserved for the nobility.[3] Part western and part Victorian in a manner, until the day she died in 2004 at the age of ninety-six Frances kept an assortment of leather work gloves for the ranch and white cotton gloves for the city.

Born November 29, 1908, at her family's two-story home in Fort Worth, Frances Elaine Rosenthal, was an only child and a second-generation Texan who appreciated the diversity in her family tree. Her father, Mose A. Rosenthal, born in 1878, was raised in Greenville, the Hunt County seat where his Russian-born father sold furniture. In Fort Worth, Mose operated the Rosenthal Furniture Company at a bustling intersection. Frances's mother, Mary Neumegen, was a Weatherford native born in 1879 and raised in Waco. Her maternal grandfather, German-born Samuel Neumegen, had grown up in England and migrated to Central Texas via San Francisco in 1867. A dry goods merchant, he married German-born, Waco-reared Rachel Marx.[4] In the early years of the century, the Neumegens moved to Fort Worth with their six daughters and two sons.

These two extended families—the Rosenthals and Neumegens—assimilated culturally and commercially into the Texas environment, though not religiously or socially. In September 1902 Mose Rosenthal, Sam Neumegen, Sam's brother-in-law Isadore Marx, and forty other Jewish men—whose wives had clout but no vote—became founding members of a synagogue named Beth-El Congregation, "Beth-El" being Hebrew for "House of God."[5] "Although Jews were not completely excluded," Frances would write many years later in the *Encyclopaedia Judaica*, "social acceptance in its highest ranks had always been limited."[6] For example, when planning whist parties and birthday celebrations, they invited other Jews, not their Christian neighbors or customers. For matchmaking opportunities, they looked to the sons, daughters, and cousins of their coreligionists.[7] Not surprisingly, in 1902 Mose Rosenthal, twenty-four, began courting Mary Neumegen, twenty-three. A year later the couple signed a marriage certificate inscribed with the Gregorian date, "15th of November 1903," and the Hebrew date, "25th of Heshvan, 5664."[8]

In those days of dirt roads and wooden sidewalks, shoppers hitched up a horse and buggy for the ride into downtown Fort Worth. By 1910, automobiles were sharing the streets. Frances later recalled her family traveling around town in a Studebaker, an indication of their financial success and modernity. "My mother was one of the first women in Fort Worth to drive," she recalled. "My mother would offer other people rides. She would say, 'I have a machine. We don't have to worry about tiring the horse.'"9

As a student in the city's public schools, Frances made the honor roll. For her senior year, her parents transferred her to St. Mary's College for Girls, a local Episcopal school. They wanted their daughter to be more academically challenged and have a better shot at one of the Seven Sisters colleges. Frances became valedictorian and in 1925 enrolled at Vassar College in Poughkeepsie, New York. While she did well scholastically, the curriculum was too limited and the student body too homogeneous for a protofeminist like Frances. Explaining why she left, she recalled: "I was not happy there. I did not like it. . . . Because at that time their courses at Vassar were very limited. . . . I transferred to the University of Chicago, and. . . . was able to branch out. I had always had a very great interest in archaeology as well as history. . . . They offered courses which I couldn't get at Vassar."10 She graduated with a degree in economics in 1929 with plans to go into banking. However, the stock market crash that October quashed those dreams. "When I graduated in 1929," she said, "the Depression came on, and there weren't banking jobs going around."11

It was a Texas custom in those days for college coeds to spend a few weeks during the summer visiting girlfriends in other towns. In each locale, the young women were feted at parties and matched with local beaus. "A visitor livened up the social scene," Frances recalled. In the summer of 1929, Bertha "Tibe" Kallison of San Antonio visited a college classmate in Fort Worth and met Frances. The following year, "on Decoration Day" (now Memorial Day), Frances's family "decided to drive to San Antonio" to visit friends and stay over at the St. Anthony Hotel.12 Frances contacted Tibe Kallison, who invited her to a Temple League picnic and swim party. The Temple League was the young adult offshoot of San Antonio's Temple Beth-El, a Reform Jewish congregation. Tibe fixed up Frances with a local fellow. During the party, however, Tibe's older brother, Perry, took notice of his sister's friend.

The next day, Perry Kallison invited Frances to the Hillcrest Country Club. During an afternoon of swimming and conversation, he was smitten. Here was a girl of intellect who was also at home in the saddle. "On the Fourth of July, Perry came up to see me in Fort Worth," Frances recalled. For Labor Day weekend, she took the overnight train to San Antonio and got her first tour of the Kallison Ranch. She fell in love with both Perry and the ranch. The couple set their wedding date for the following March. The ceremony would be in San Antonio rather than Fort Worth because Perry's father, Nathan Kallison, had suffered a paralytic stroke. On March 8, 1931, Rabbi Ephraim Frisch married Perry and Frances in the parlor of the King Ranch Suite at the Menger Hotel. For their honeymoon, the couple traveled by Pullman car to Mexico City before beginning their life together in San Antonio.[13]

Frances stepped into a new world. The Kallison family enterprises revolved around a downtown farm-and-ranch store that stretched up and down a city block. Their 2,700-acre ranch had show horses, prize-winning bulls, and fields of experimental crops.[14] Patriarch Nathan Kallison, a harness maker, had launched his business three decades before in a twenty-by-twenty-foot workshop. He had been born in 1873 in Ladyzhinka, a shtetl in the Ukraine, and as a boy was apprenticed to a leatherworker who cut, tanned, and stitched bridles and harnesses. At age seventeen, Nathan fled Russia to escape "marauding Cossacks . . . hell-bent on slaughtering Jews."[15] When he settled in Chicago in 1890, he possessed the skills that would earn him a livelihood. In 1895 he married Anna Letwin, a Ukrainian immigrant from Kiev. Due to her fragile health, the couple moved in 1899 to San Antonio, then Texas's largest city with 53,300 residents.[16]

Six years later, with profits from the saddlery, the Kallisons did something forbidden to Jews in their native country. They purchased land—ranchland twenty miles northwest of San Antonio, just inside the county line. The property was on the Culebra Road, a frontier supply route blazed by military scouts in the 1850s. The core of the property had belonged to descendants of the Hoffmans, the German family that had homesteaded the acreage. Before them, nomadic Apache and Comanche tribes left arrowheads, blades of tomahawks, and shards of

clay pots that became embedded in the earth. The property was pris-
tine rural real estate. In springtime, if the May rains were plentiful,
the ranch became lush with mountain laurel, juniper, black cherry, chi-
naberry, and live oak trees. Year round it was habitat for rabbit, deer,
boar, and turkey. Eagles soared overhead. Lurking in the brush were
rattlers and copperheads. On this fertile acreage, a farmer could drill
a well, construct a windmill, and tap into fresh groundwater from the
Edwards Aquifer far below.

Whenever a neighboring property went on the market, the Kallisons
added to their holdings. They assembled a small herd of cattle, setting
aside roughly half the land for pasture and half for feed crops. As a
newcomer to agribusiness, the Kallison Ranch was open to experimen-
tation. The conventional wisdom was that wheat, a cold-weather crop,
could not flourish in Bexar County. The Kallisons, however, found
success with Abyssinian Duran wheat, a species that proved hardy
enough to grow in South Texas.[17]

As the horse gave way to the internal-combustion engine, the
Kallisons' harness-and-saddle shop branched into hardware, tractors,
lumber, barbed wire, branding irons, and western wear. Anna and
Nathan Kallison spent Monday through Saturday in the city minding
the store and Sundays at the ranch, conferring with the manager and
hired hands who lived on the premises. Sunday was also ranching day
for their children—two sons and two daughters. Running the ranch
fell largely to Perry, particularly after his father's stroke. With Frances
as his partner and confidante, he contracted with an itinerant builder,
T. R. Stephenson, to construct a house of native stone on the north
end of the property. The dwelling had indoor plumbing and was wired
for electricity, comforts that optimists like Perry and Frances believed
were coming to rural America. The ranch manager lived in the house.
Some years later the couple designed a larger, contemporary ranch
house for themselves. The dwelling, also constructed of limestone,
featured broad casement windows, a double-sided fireplace, two bed-
rooms, and a large kitchen. The family dubbed their country cottage
the "rock house." With its large screened-in porch and views of the
Hill Country, the dwelling became a gathering place for politicians,
dove hunters, and overnight guests for years to come.

Figure 16. Frances Kallison
at Kallison Ranch, 1930s.
From the collection of Nick
Kotz.

Frances and Perry always had business on their minds, even during vacations. In 1935 the couple drove to Colorado for a month-long sojourn. As they motored through New Mexico with its vast expanses of land, the only signs of commerce were a trading post here and there. That gave Perry an idea. "When we got back to San Antonio, he told me he thought that a radio program, called 'The Trading Post,' would be a good way to advertise the farm-and-ranch store," Frances recalled, adding, "Remember, this is before television. The show would offer for sale or trade anything that anybody had to sell. They could advertise it, free, i.e., 'John M. needs to buy a good used tractor.' Or 'Joe S. wants to sell a bull.'"[18]

Radio station KTSA bought into the idea, and *The Trading Post*, a fifteen-minute early-morning broadcast, debuted in 1935, the start of a forty-six-year run. Initially a professional radio announcer anchored the show, but the fellow was inclined to the bottle. "One morning,"

Frances recalled, "he was too drunk to put a program on." Perry stepped up to the microphone. Affecting the cadence of a rural rancher, he launched into a fast-moving monologue, relaying market reports, cattle prices, improvements in grass seed, and upcoming social events such as the Helotes Volunteer Firemen's Barbecue. Like an auctioneer, he ticked off the names and hometowns of customers who had dropped by the store the previous day. As he joked about seeds and weeds and rhymed "rodeo" (pronounced *ROAD-ya*) with *San An-TON-ya*, a new radio personality was born—Perry Kallison, the "Ol' Trader."[19]

Traffic at the store multiplied. Customers signed their names in a cloth-bound ledger and jotted down items to sell or trade on the radio. They made note of recent births, graduations, and upcoming anniversaries. Listeners knew that the Kallison Ranch tested new products and won awards for soil conservation. That made them all the more eager to trek into town for a word with the radio rancher. A fresh pot of coffee was always percolating at the store. There was no charge for a cup of brew, although it was suggested that folks drop donations into the "coffee pipeline." The coins went for good causes, such as an iron lung for Samantha "Sammy" Franklin, a farmer's daughter in Poteet who was fighting polio.[20]

At the Kallison home on Sanford Drive, the phone rang throughout dinner and into the evening. Often it was an undertaker with news of a death, asking the Ol' Trader to broadcast the time and location of a funeral. The Ol' Trader saved such sad tidings for the closing moments of his broadcasts, announcing in solemn tones that "Bill Hastings of Canyon Springs has *gone away*." Then he would tell listeners where to pay their last respects. In short order, the radio show became a public service, a communications link that connected ranches beyond the reach of telephone lines and newspaper delivery routes. The broadcasts also helped the Kallisons' business grow.

Yet all around them Frances observed the Great Depression's toll. "There were a lot of people living in tents—Hoovervilles—on the outskirts of the city." The extended family's involvement in both urban and agricultural affairs paved the way for Frances's own brand of activism, which evolved after her marriage to Perry in 1931. Her concern drew her to the San Antonio section of the National Council of Jewish Women (NCJW) because of its advocacy for social-welfare programs. By 1938 she was the group's local president. Medical care for poor people, particularly women and children, topped her agenda. San Antonio's public hospital had no maternity ward. With a delegation from the council, Frances visited the mayor's office to "plead for a maternity ward at the Robert B. Green Hospital." With her minions, Frances became instrumental in its creation. The council also established a well-baby clinic and a prenatal clinic—"one of the first in the city," according to Frances. Her New Deal advocacy didn't end there. At NCJW state conventions she argued for repeal of Texas's $2.50 poll tax, "because it kept the poor from voting." Her reference was to the region's marginalized Hispanics and African Americans. Frances's leadership expanded during 1940s when she served as a regional council officer from 1941 to 1946 and president of the council's Texas-Oklahoma-Colorado region from 1946 to 1949. Such lobbying presaged core issues of the civil rights movement and the feminist era that came to the fore decades later.[21]

Following World War II, Frances was on the ground floor of another emerging local institution—the Ladies' Auxiliary to the Bexar County Sheriff's Mounted Posse, a riding club for ranching women with the "common desire to promote superb horsemanship, perfection of mounted drills, and good sportsmanship." The Ladies' Posse formed in October 1947 and rapidly became a popular public attraction because of its novelty and expertise. In April 1948 the posse won a blue ribbon in the San Antonio Fiesta's Western Parade. It became a fixture on the San Antonio Livestock Exposition's opening day. Each October the equestrian group celebrated its birthday with drill team exhibitions, performing for soldiers at the army's Brooke General Hospital, polio patients at the public hospital, and children at local orphanages. One of these anniversary exhibitions, staged along with a fair at Brackenridge Park, drew three thousand people. "The celebration was not to be a selfish one," Frances wrote in a colorful article published in the *Cattleman*, the magazine of the Texas and Southwestern Cattle Raisers Association. "Its financial success enabled the ladies' group to donate a physiotherapy machine to the polio ward of the Robert B. Green Hospital and $200 to the San Antonio Community Chest, in addition to numerous other services and philanthropies." Combining ranch life with public service and empowering women was what motivated Frances.[22]

Initially the Ladies' Posse was intended as an auxiliary in the traditional, sexist sense—a distaff group formed in support of husbands—but it soon eclipsed the masculine riders. As Frances wrote: "Although the wives of the Posse members were organized to assist their husbands in every way in their projects, the girls soon developed a crack drill team of their own." Rather than restrict the auxiliary to spouses, membership was expanded to include "mothers, sisters, daughters or sweethearts of Posse members or, with each man entitled to sponsor one lady of his choice." The women gained celebrity status when their posse appeared on camera during the San Antonio filming of two motion pictures: *Two Guys from Texas* (1948) and *Rio Grande* (1950), starring John Wayne and Maureen O'Hara. The posse was also filmed in an episode of television's *The Cisco Kid*. Aside from the "glamour," Frances wrote, "these horsewomen . . . enjoy the thought that they have some small part in preserving the spirit and tradition of the true old Southwest."[23]

One afternoon at the ranch, Frances was paying a traveling blacksmith when the two realized they had met when she was a child. The horseshoer was Tom Bibb. He had shod her father's dray horses before World War I. Still plying his trade in the 1940s and 1950s, Bibb operated a mobile blacksmith shop from the back of his pickup, driving from ranch to ranch and stable to stable. Frances realized Bibb's narrative was a piece of fading history worth recording. In a 1957 article published in the *Cattleman*, she related that he was likely the last of his line: "His grandfather [migrated] from France to Georgia about 1810. . . . The family had been blacksmiths for generations and continued their trade in the New World. The family moved westward to Texas and Tom was born in Derango [Durango], near Temple, in 1896. His father farmed a bit and operated the town smithy. Young Tom learned horseshoeing as his father's assistant. In 1910 the family moved to Fort Worth, where the father and son shod the dray horses of many of the still well known businesses, among them the Binyon-O'Keefe."[24] In 1912, when Frances was four, Tom Bibb had begun to shoe the dray horses for her father's Rosenthal Furniture Company. In the 1940s and 1950s he had regularly shod Frances's pleasure mare, her eldest daughter Maryann's pony, and her youngest daughter Bobbi's three-gaited show mare.

The Kallison daughters were such promising riders that Perry and Frances looked into sending them to Camp Waldemar in Hunt, Texas, where a number of their girlfriends benefited from summer riding lessons. Waldemar, however, was restricted, meaning that it was closed to Jews. The camp director privately told Perry and Frances that Waldemar would make an exception for their daughters. The family chafed at such selective discrimination. They did not want tokenism, much less favoritism stemming from their status in the ranching community. Rather, they expected equal treatment for all. Since that was not forthcoming, the Kallison girls attended Camp Mystic, a Hill Country camp three miles from Hunt, which was open to all.[25]

The Kallison Ranch's agricultural network became international in 1964 when the Israeli Ministry of Agriculture sent two young men to Texas A&M University to research the feasibility of raising Angora goats at Kibbutz Yodfat, a rocky area in the Lower Galilee. The climate and terrain of Israel, where goats had flourished since ancient times, was similar to South Texas. With Angoras came the potential for a lucrative mohair industry. Extension agents at Texas A&M referred the Israeli visitors to the Kallisons, who were eager to introduce them to South Texas goat ranchers. First, however, they took the Israelis for a shopping spree at the Big Country Kallison Store to outfit them with blue jeans, boots, hand-tooled leather belts, and bolo ties. Recalled Frances, "Jews and non-Jews who were sympathetic to Israel donated goats" and cash, enabling the Israelis to assemble a herd of seventy-six Angora kids.[26]

Initially the goats fared so well that one of the Israelis returned the next year with money from the Ministry of Agriculture to purchase 250 more Angoras.[27] Traveling with him was his new bride. The Kallisons put up the newlyweds in the stone cottage at the ranch and hosted a honeymoon party—replete with tents, barbecued beef, beer, wine, liquor, and cockfights in three arenas. "Despite the sport's illegal status . . . none of the law enforcement officers in attendance registered any objection."[28] In December 1967, just before Israeli prime minister Levi Eshkol visited the LBJ Ranch, Perry briefed President Lyndon Johnson, whom the Kallisons had known since LBJ's days as a Texas congressman, on the Angora goat project.[29]

Frances had a passion for local history. Fascinated with the ethnic mix integral to America's western heritage, she made it her goal to research, publicize, and popularize the history of the Jews of Texas. In 1954 she cochaired San Antonio's American Jewish Tercentenary Committee, which commemorated three hundred years of organized Jewry in America. In 1966 she was appointed to the board of the American Jewish Historical Society, then headquartered in Boston.

That same year, R. Henderson Schuffler, a friend of Governor John B. Connally, requested that she gather materials for an ethnic Jewish exhibit at the Texas Pavilion of HemisFair, the world's fair slated to open in San Antonio in 1968. The fair's theme was "Confluence of Civilizations in the Americas." The Texas Pavilion's first floor was envisioned as an interactive museum of the state's ethnic groups. Frances embarked with gusto on this mission, traveling to communities and libraries across the state to interview people and gather documents and artifacts.

While planning the exhibit, Frances met with opposition from unexpected quarters. Two rabbis—including the spiritual leader at her own Temple Beth-El in San Antonio—wrote letters insisting that Judaism was not a culture but a religion, analogous to a branch of Protestantism, and ought not be included in the cultural exhibit.[30] Frances argued persuasively with organizers of the Texas Pavilion that Judaism embodied an ancient culture with distinctive holidays, rituals, foods, literature, and ongoing traditions that positively impacted the development of the larger Texas community. Although the number of Texas Jews was relatively small (a mere six-tenths of 1 percent of the populace), Jewish settlers had comprised a distinct segment of the population since the Lone Star Republic's inception in 1836. They had fought with the Army of the Republic of Texas; they had been among the founders of Waco and San Angelo; they had driven herds up the Chisholm Trail; during oil booms, they had pioneered the pipe-and-supply industry. They had been trailblazers in the mercantile arena and pacesetters in

Figure 17. Maryann, Frances, and Pete Kallison, 1940s.
From the collection of Nick Kotz.

the state's civil rights movement. Frances successfully argued that Texas Jewish history deserved to be spotlighted along with the Native American, Czech, Polish, German, Norwegian, and Canary Island cultures in the exhibit.[31] She prevailed.[32]

Harsh times, economic downturns, and ill health were simultaneously affecting the Kallison family. Perry's older brother Morris, a politician and real estate tycoon, died unexpectedly in 1966 at the age of seventy. His extended family was left with unfinished projects on the drawing board and outstanding loans.[33] The family's farm-and-ranch store experienced a decline in business. Denim and western wear became such fashion staples that the Kallisons' rural customers could shop for their clothing at suburban malls. Big-box stores began opening on previously vacant rural highways, eliminating the need for ranchers to drive into San Antonio for goods and conversation. Kallison's Trading Post, with its payroll of 125 employees, was losing money.

In 1967 the Kallisons' extended family, which jointly owned the downtown store and the Bexar County ranch, was forced to liquidate and downsize. Overnight, an out-of-state firm auctioned off the goods in the store. Perry and Frances Kallison's two hundred prized Polled Herefords, including a bull that had just won the reserve championship at the San Antonio Livestock Show, were also auctioned. The acreage on the edge of the Bexar County was leased to ranchers running cattle and to hunters during dove and deer season. Perry and his son Pete opened a small western store near the Alamo. As evidence that the Kallison name still had cachet, Princess Grace and Prince Rainier of Monaco visited the downsized store in 1968.[34]

Perry had by then moved his radio studio into his home in the city. San Antonio's KMAC aired the show and relayed the signal to a network of outlying stations. Hundreds of rural listeners tuned in, but, with changing times and habits, fewer San Antonio commuters were interested. They preferred traffic reports. The show went off the air April 26, 1981. By then the Ol' Trader's hands were shaky. Parkinson's disease kept him at home. On February 13, 1999, after sixty-seven years of marriage, Perry Kallison died at the age of ninety-five.[35]

By then Frances was entrenched in researching Texas Jewish history. During the decade following HemisFair, she had gone back to school and earned a master's degree from Trinity University when she was sixty-nine. Her thesis, titled "100 Years of Jewry in San Antonio," substantiated her contention that "the arrival of Jews parallels the history of other ethnic groups in Texas cities."[36] A shorter essay, with the intriguing title "Was It a Duel or a Murder? A Study in Texan Assimilation," was published in the *American Jewish Historical Quarterly*, gaining her attention among scholars in the field. The piece begins in San Antonio's oldest Jewish cemetery, where the inscription on a tombstone reveals that the deceased had died a violent death. Frances

mused over the inscription, found newspapers and diaries that speculated on the conflict that led to the man's end, and tracked down the
life stories of his friends and enemies. As Frances pieced together the
tale, she concluded: "It demonstrates how quickly the Jews who were
bold enough to come to the frontier became assimilated into the mores
of the society in which they lived."[37]

In 1979 Galveston rabbi James L. Kessler enlisted Frances's help
organizing the Texas Jewish Historical Society (TJHS).[38] The two
were not acquainted, but the rabbi was familiar with her credentials.
"In a day and age when the history of Texas Jews . . . was not register-
ing in anyone's thoughts, this topic was all consuming for Frances,"
he later explained.[39] At an organizing conference in San Antonio
attended by 150 people in March 1980, the rabbi was elected president, with Frances Kallison his first vice president and successor as
president from 1982 to 1984. "Frances gave the Society credibility
and legitimized its presence in the community," the rabbi said. "She
allowed her stature among regional historians to be transferred to the
budding efforts of the TJHS," which by the turn of the century had
grown to more than one thousand members.[40]

The Kallison name is no longer attached to a radio show, a San
Antonio store, or a Bexar County ranch. In 2002 Texas's Government
Canyon State Natural Area expanded its boundaries to incorporate
1,162 acres of the Kallison family property. The Texas Parks and Wildlife Commission, with dollars from the federal Land and Water Conservation Fund and the City of San Antonio, using bond money, paid a
total of $5.8 million for it.[41] The acreage was deemed ecologically vital
because of its location above the recharge zone of the Edwards Aquifer,
the water source for the region. Frances found comfort in the fact that
the land the Kallisons had long tended and conserved was appraised as
invaluable to the region's future health. Since then, visitors to the area
have hiked miles of trails, climbed scenic vistas, explored spring-fed
creeks, and even observed the golden-cheeked warbler, an endangered
species.[42]

Despite Frances's senior status, or perhaps because of it, historians,
social activists, and researchers made pilgrimages to her San Antonio
home for strategy sessions on civic issues and to record her recollec-

tions. California novelist Nina Vida credited Frances as the inspiration for her 2006 novel *The Texicans*. "Until I met Frances Kallison," she wrote, "I didn't know whether the world needed another book about Texas, but she took me by the hand and told me about her grandparents, who settled in Texas in the 1870s, about her mother, . . . one of the first women in Fort Worth to drive a car, and about the western goods store and . . . cattle ranch her husband's family owned. . . . Frances was an intrepid booster and devoted historian . . . as at home on a horse as she was at a white-glove tea."[43]

In 2016, twelve years after her death, Frances Rosenthal Kallison was tapped for induction into the National Cowgirl Museum and Hall of Fame, its first Jewish honoree. The hall of fame's mission is to honor and "document the lives of women who have distinguished themselves while exemplifying the pioneer spirit of the American West." Frances Kallison did just that. She left her imprint on the land, helping manage the family ranch, which was ultimately incorporated into a state natural area. She left her stamp at the Institute of Texan Cultures, research-ing and arguing for inclusion of an exhibit about the Jews of Texas. Everything Frances Kallison did, from organizing the women's posse to her grassroots social work in San Antonio, demonstrates that she was a trailblazer forging a path for others. In the equestrian arena, she set high standards for dress, drill, and civic-mindedness. Her published writing, geared to both popular audiences and academicians, brought insights about ranch life, riding, and religion to the fore. She was ahead of her time. Her legacy continues.

Notes

1. Frances R. Kallison, "Tom Bibb . . . Blacksmith to Three Generations," *Cattleman*, September 1957, 148.

2. Frances R, Kallison, interview with author, San Antonio, January 7, 1996.

3. Frances R. Kallison, interview with Helen Wilk, transcript, Texas Jewish Historical Society Collection, Briscoe Center for American History, University of Texas at Austin (hereafter TJHS Collection).

4. U.S. Census, Texas, 1910, 1920, 1930; Kallison interview with author.

5. Hollace Ava Weiner, *Beth-El Congregation Centennial: Fort Worth, Texas, 1902–2002* (Fort Worth: Beth-El Congregation, 2000), 6–12.

6. "Jews have been cordially accepted in all phases of industrial, commercial, and professional life in San Antonio. However, social acceptance in its highest

ranks has always been limited, although Jews have not been completely excluded." Among the prominent leaders named in the article were the Oppenheimer family of pioneer bankers, ranchers, and Confederate veterans; the Halff family of ranchers; Max Reiter, founder of the San Antonio Symphony Orchestra; and Frances's spouse, Perry Kallison, whom she cited as an "agriculturalist and local radio personality." Frances Rosenthal Kallison, "San Antonio," in *Encyclopaedia Judaica* (Jerusalem: Keter Publishing House, 1972).

7. Hollace Ava Weiner, "Tied and Tethered (*'Geknippt und Gebinden'*): Jews in Early Fort Worth," *Southwestern Historical Quarterly* 57, no. 3 (January 2004): 389–414. See also social columns of *Southwest Jewish Sentiment* (Dallas), August 16, October 4, October 25, November 22, December 6, December 20, 1901, and February 7, 1902.

8. Marriage Certificate, Oversized Box 1, Fort Worth Jewish Archives at Beth-El Congregation.

9. Kallison interview with author.

10. Ibid.

11. Ibid.

12. Ibid. Bertha was nicknamed "Birdie," which morphed into "Tibe," pronounced *Tibby*, the Yiddish diminutive of Elizabeth.

13. Ibid. A seven-course champagne dinner followed the marriage ceremony. Docia Schultz Williams, *History and Mystery of the Menger Hotel* (Dallas: Republic of Texas Press, 2000), 118–20; Hollace Ava Weiner, "Evolution and Dissolution of a Pulpit: Ephraim and Ruth Cohen Frisch, San Antonio," in *Jewish Stars in Texas: Rabbis and Their Work* (College Station: Texas A&M University Press, 1999), 156–81.

14. The Kallisons' ranching success wasn't unprecedented among Texas Jews. See Patrick Dearen, *Halff of Texas: Merchant Rancher of the Old West* (Austin: Eakin Press, 2000); Patrick Dearen, "Home on the Range: Mayer Halff's Cattle Empire," in *Lone Stars of David: The Jews of Texas*, ed. Hollace Ava Weiner and Kenneth D. Roseman (Waltham, Mass.: Brandeis University Press, 2007), 50–63.

15. Nick Kotz, "Enduring Legacy," *Texas Parks and Wildlife*, August–September 2014, accessed June 20, 2016, http://www.tpwmagazine.com/archive/2014/aug/LLL_govtcanyon.

16. Nick Kotz, *The Harness Maker's Dream: Nathan Kallison and the Rise of South Texas* (Fort Worth: Texas Christian University Press, 2013), 5, 12, 13.

17. Tom McGowan, "Man of Word, Says Son: Morris Kallison's Dad Laid Groundwork for 'Empire,'" *San Antonio Light*, ca. December 1962, clipping in TJHS Collection; "Kallison, Nathan," obituary, *Cattleman*, January 1945, 90.

18. Kallison interview with author.

19. Perry Kallison, interview with Frances R. Kallison, July 18, 1976, transcript, TJHS Collection; *Kallison's Trading Post—The Cow Country News*, KMAC-Radio, cassette tape recording, 1960, in possession of Nick Kotz, Broad Run, Virginia. The latter includes Perry Kallison interview with entertainer Jimmie Dean.

20. *Kallison's Trading Post—The Cow Country News*, KMAC-Radio, cassette tape recording, 1960.

21. Kallison oral history, 1991, TJHS Collection; Kallison interview with author.

22. Mrs. Perry Kallison, "The Ladies' Auxiliary to the Bexar County Sheriff's Mounted Posse," *Cattleman*, September 1951, 124–26, 128. The term "posse" denotes a vigilante police detachment riding en masse on horseback in search of an outlaw. As the Wild West became tame, posses evolved into sociable riding clubs that participated in ceremonial parades.

23. Ibid. The article described how the riders dressed in "smart light blue serge trousers and shirts, with a darker blue yoke." They accented their outfits with white western hats, white gloves, and "flag-red ties" and spruced up each horse with a red-and-white saddle corona.

24. Frances R. Kallison, "Tom Bibb . . . Blacksmith to Three Generations," *Cattleman*, September 1957, 148. Binyon O'Keefe was still in business in 2016 as Binyon O'Keefe Hudson, a moving-and-storage company.

25. "Camp Waldemar didn't take Jews, but the man told my Dad, 'We would take your girls.'" Maryann Kallison Friedman, interview with author, May 20, 2003. Another possible example of anti-Semitism was Frances Kallison's exclusion from local garden clubs. An accomplished green thumb, Frances crossbred flowering plants in her San Antonio garden, yet she never received an invitation to join a ladies' garden club, "nor was her home ever included in the city's prestigious annual Garden Tour. Her daughters resented their mother's exclusion, suspecting it came . . . from a policy of excluding Jews, from simple social snobbery, or both." Nick Kotz, *Harness Maker's Dream*, 205. According to a 2016 newspaper article, "Her family sometimes was turned away from lodges or riding camps that did not welcome Jews. When the movie *Driving Miss Daisy*, about a Jewish woman and her black driver, was released in 1989, Kallison walked out of the theater after the first forty-five minutes because 'it hit too close to home,' her daughter said. 'But that sort of thing rolled off her. She didn't make a cause out of it. . . . She faced prejudice at times but did it with grace,' [Bobbi Kallison] Ravicz said." Scott Huddleston, "National Honor for Rancher Kallison," *San Antonio Express-News*, September 26, 2016.

26. Letter from Yoram and Ruti Avidor to Nick Kotz, December 14, 2008, and letter to ranchers, quoted in Kotz, *Harness Maker's Dream*, 232–33; Kallison interviews.

27. Ida M. Barkan, "Israel Helped by Texan in New Goat Industry," *National Jewish Post and Opinion*, January 8, 1965, referenced in Kotz, *Harness Maker's Dream*, 232. The goats were purchased from the Uvalde ranch of Dolph Briscoe, Texas governor in 1973–79.

28. Kotz, *Harness Maker's Dream*, 231–34.

29. Perry Kallison to Lyndon Baines Johnson, December 29, 1967, Ex GI 2–11/A-Z, WHCF, LBJ Presidential Library, Austin, Texas, quoted in Kotz, *Harness Maker's Dream*, 234.

30. Kallison interview with author.

31. At the core of the disagreement are two ideological frameworks for understanding Judaism. One separates the sacred from the secular and views Judaism as a religion, akin to the Lutheran or Methodist faith; the other views Jews as a people who self-identify through religion, culture, traditions, teachings, holidays, and literature. See Weiner, "The Celebrity Rabbi, or Splintering over Zionism," in *Jewish Stars in Texas*, 159; Karl Preuss, "David Jacobson and the Integration of San Antonio," in *The Quiet Voices: Southern Rabbis and Black Civil Rights, 1800s to 1990s*, ed. Mark K. Bauman and Berkley Kalin (Tuscaloosa: University of Alabama Press, 1997), 135–51.

32. When HemisFair closed, the Texas Pavilion was renamed the Institute of Texan Cultures. It became part of the University of Texas at San Antonio, where it flourishes as a museum and library visited by busloads of school children. The institute's first-floor exhibit space is periodically updated. By 2016 it recognized more than twenty-five nationalities and cultural communities across Texas.

33. "Morris Kallison, Businessman, Dies," *San Antonio Express*, February 21, 1966, TJHS Collection.

34. Princess Grace and Prince Rainier III of Monaco bought boots and cowboy hats while in San Antonio for HemisFair. "Western Wear, History Fill Kallison's Shelves," *San Antonio Express-News*, August 15, 1989; Kotz, *Harness Maker's Dream*, 249.

35. Carmina Danini, "Longtime 'Trading Post' Host Kallison Dies at 95," *San Antonio Express-News*, February 14, 1999; "Senate Resolution No. 430 in Memory of Perry Kallison," Texas State Senate, March 16, 1999.

36. "The first Jews to arrive were adventurers, seeking land grants, economic benefits, and a love of freedom. . . . These early arrivals chose the Southwest frontier because of the social mobility there, as much as the economic opportunities offered. . . . These were men and women willing to break with old patterns of life and to adopt new ones. . . . There could not have been general prejudice against them. Frances R. Kallison, "100 Years of Jewry in San Antonio" (master's thesis, Trinity University, San Antonio, 1977).

37. Frances Kallison, "Was It a Duel or a Murder? A Study in Texan Assimilation," *American Jewish Historical Quarterly* 62 (March 1972: 312–20), reprinted in *Western States Jewish History* 27 (1995): 254–62; Betty Hilton, "Frances Kallison: Historian—Sleuth," *San Antonio Jewish Journal*, circa May 1973, clipping, Kallison file, Institute of Texan Cultures, San Antonio.

38. James Lee "Jimmy" Kessler served thirty-two years as rabbi at Galveston's Temple B'nai Israel. Born December 10, 1945, in Houston, Kessler received a BA from the University of Texas at Austin and was ordained in 1972, with a degree from Hebrew Union College, Jewish Institute of Religion. In the American Jewish Archives (AJA), located on the Cincinnati campus of Hebrew Union, he obtained access to files relating to a controversy at his boyhood congregation, Houston's Beth Israel Congregation. See James Lee Kessler, "A Study of the Split of Congregation Beth Israel, Houston, Texas, 1942–22," manuscript, 1971, American Jewish Archives, Hebrew Union College, Cincinnati.

39. Jimmy Kessler, "Frances Kallison (1908–2004)," 26th Annual Gathering, Texas Jewish Historical Society, Austin, Texas, April 9, 2005.

40. Ibid.; Frances Kallison oral history transcript, TJHS Collection.

41. "Acreage Added to Government Canyon State Natural Area," Texas Parks and Wildlife, press release, July 1, 2002.

42. Kotz, "Enduring Legacy."

43. Nina Vida, *The Texicans* (New York: Soho Press, 2006), v.

Contributors

John T. "Jack" Becker is a librarian with Texas Tech University Libraries and works with TTU Department of History faculty and students. His reading, writing, and research interests cover a wide area, including cattle ranching, Native American history, the American Southwest, the art of Georgia O'Keeffe, agriculture, and the Civil War era. Becker has written, edited, and coauthored several books and many book chapters and journal articles. He lives on the western edge of Lubbock with his wife, Cindy, where they enjoy reading, gardening, cycling, and taking care of their two horses.

Light Townsend Cummins retired in 2018 as the Guy M. Bryan Professor of History at Austin College in Sherman, Texas, where he had been a member of the faculty since 1978. Among his fourteen books are *A Guide to the History of Louisiana* (1988), *A Guide to the History of Texas* (1988), *Spanish Observers and the American Revolution, 1775–1783* (1992), and his coauthored *Louisiana: A History* (2014). He is the author of several dozen scholarly articles dealing with the Gulf Coast, Louisiana, and Texas. Cummins was a Fulbright scholar to Spain in 1975–76, serves as an associate of the Danforth Foundation, and is a former member of the board of directors of the Texas Council for the Humanities. He is a lifetime fellow of the Texas State Historical Association, former president of the Southwestern Historical Association and of the Louisiana Historical Association, and has been active in a number of other historical organizations. Recent books are *Discovering Texas History* and *On History's Trail: Speeches and Essays of the Texas State Historian, 2009–2012*. His *Allie Victoria Tennent and the Visual Arts in Dallas* won the Liz Carpenter Award.

Alex Hunt is Haley Professor of Western Studies and professor of English at West Texas A&M University. He is the founding director of the Center for the Study of the American West and outgoing editor of the *Panhandle-Plains Historical Review*. Hunt's last book was an edited republication of Townshend and Hyde's *Our Indian Summer in the Far West*, a British travel narrative of 1879, with University of Oklahoma Press. Hunt is a lifelong resident and lover of the American West.

Renee M. Laegreid, PhD, is professor of history, US West, at the University of Wyoming. Her area of specialty is women and gender in the twentieth-century West, and her publications include *Riding Pretty: Rodeo Royalty in the American West* (2006), an exploration of the emergence and development of the rodeo queen phenomena from 1909 to 1969, and a coedited volume of essays, *Women on the North American Plains* (2011), that provides an overview of the diversity of women and their experiences in this region. She has published numerous essays on ranch women and rodeo and is series editor for Women, Gender, and the West, a book series published by Texas Tech University Press.

Deborah M. Liles received her PhD at the University of North Texas in 2013. She is an assistant professor at Tarleton State University and holds the W. K. Gordon Endowed Chair of Texas History. Her publications include *Women in Civil War Texas: Diversity and Dissidence in the Trans-Mississippi*, coedited with Angela Boswell and winner of the 2016 Liz Carpenter Award; *African Americans in Central Texas*, coedited with Bruce A. Glasrud; and the forthcoming *Southern Roots, Western Foundations: The Livestock Industry and Slavery*, which examines the connections between successful slave owners and the livestock industry.

Amy M. Porter received her PhD from Southern Methodist University, and she is an associate professor of history at Texas A&M University–San Antonio. Her book *Their Lives, Their Wills: Women in the Borderlands, 1750–1846* (2015) won the Lou Halsell Rodenberger Book Prize from Texas Tech University Press and was a cowinner of the Fabiola Cabeza de Baca prize from the Historical Society of New Mexico.

Jean A. Stuntz earned her PhD from the University of North Texas and is now a Regents Professor of History at West Texas A&M University. Her first book, *Hers, His, and Theirs: Community Property Law in Spain and Early Texas*, won several awards. Stuntz has written three chapters for books that won the Liz Carpenter Award for Best Book on Women in Texas, among other awards. Her current research is on the pioneer women of the Texas Panhandle.

Cecilia Gutierrez Venable has worked in archives for more than twenty years. She also taught history courses at several universities. Venable received her BA and MA from Texas A&M University–Corpus Christi. Currently she is working on her PhD at the University of Texas at El Paso. Venable has authored several books and articles and is now the historian and director of archives for the Sisters of the Holy Spirit and Mary Immaculate.

Hollace Ava Weiner is the author of *Jewish Stars in Texas: Rabbis and Their Work* (1999), *Jewish "Junior League": The Rise and Fall of the Fort Worth Council of Jewish Women* (2008), and centennial histories of two Fort Worth institutions: *Beth-El Congregation* (2002) and *River Crest Country Club* (2011). She edited the anthology *Lone Stars of David* (2007) and contributed to *Quiet Voices: Southern Rabbis and Black Civil Rights* (1997), *Dixie Diaspora* (2006), and *Grace and Gumption: Stories of Fort Worth Women* (2007). A past president of the Southern Jewish Historical Society, she is volunteer coordinator of the Fort Worth Jewish Archives.

Brooke Wibracht is a PhD candidate in the AddRan History and Geography Department at Texas Christian University. Wibracht graduated from Texas A&M University with her BA in 2004 and from Loyola University Chicago with her MA in 2011. Her dissertation modernizes the Texas Fence Cutting War by including race, class, and gender.

Index

Vida, Nina, 155
Villa de San Fernando de Béxar, 10, 15
Villa, Pancho, 133

Waco, TX, 142, 151
Wadsworth, Cornelia. *See* Adair,
 Cornelia
Wadsworth, James W., Jr., *See* Wad-
 sworth, James Wolcott, Jr.
Wadsworth, James Wolcott, Jr., 50, 51,
 54, 61
Walker, Felix, 27
Walker, George F., 49
Walker, Lucinda, 7, 25, 27, 36
Walsh, Richard "Dick", 47, 49–50, 55,
 60
Ware Ranch, 117
Warm Springs Foundation, 86
Washington County, TN, 65
Weatherford, TX, 142
Webb, Walter Prescott, 2
Weekly Herald, 95
Wellesley, Courtenay E., 59

Wetsel, Mrs. W. W., 72
Wheeler County, TX, 72
White Deer Land Company, 52
Whitfield, N. J., 110
Wilderado, TX, 111, 112, 115
Wild Horse Desert, 131
Wilson County, TX, 9
Wilson, Mrs. E. M., 72
Wilson, President Woodrow, 133
Winegarten, Ruthe, 4
women, land owned by, 9, 10, 11,
 13–14, 16, 18–20, 30–31, 42, 49,
 52–54, 58–60, 91–92, 94, 102, 107,
 122, 126, 128
Wood, Mrs. E. J., 72
World War I, 51, 79, 135
World War II, 2, 81, 115, 118, 141,
 148
Worthington, Jackie, 121

Young County, TX, 36

Zapata, TX, 137